Understanding Geography

Map Skills and Our World

Level 5

©2006 Maps.com, 120 Cremona Drive, Suite H, Santa Barbara, CA 93117 / 800-929-4MAP / 805-685-3100

ISBN 1-930194-23-4

Visit the world's premier map website at http://www.maps.com for thousands of map resources, including driving directions, address finding, and downloadable maps.

Table of Contents

Activity 10
Change Over Time: The Example of New Orleans
Use maps and graphs to learn about a large city and how it has changed over the years.

Activity 11
Immigration
Use maps and graphs to learn about patterns of immigration in the United States.

Activity 12
Growing to Fifty States
Explore how the United States of America grew from the original thirteen colonies to today's fifty states.

Activity 13
Our Nation's Capital
Look into the history and design of our nation's capital, Washington, D.C.

Activity 14
Regions
Learn about the distinct features of different regions in the United States.

Map Review
Try these exercises to review what you have learned.

Glossary

ATLAS

3

Activity 1 — The Earth on Maps and Globes

Key Words: distortion, projection, map key, compass rose, cardinal directions, intermediate directions

Imagine that you peel an orange and keep the peel in one piece. Then you press the peel flat—what happens? It bends and breaks. The only way you can flatten the peel and keep it in one piece is to stretch it. But that stretching causes **distortion**—the peel gets twisted and bent away from its true size and shape.

Like an orange, a globe is round. That's obvious, but important. Why? Because a round globe is the most accurate way to show the round Earth. On a globe all the continents are the same shape as they are on the Earth. Also, each continent is the correct size in relation to the others. There is no distortion, because a globe is shaped like the Earth.

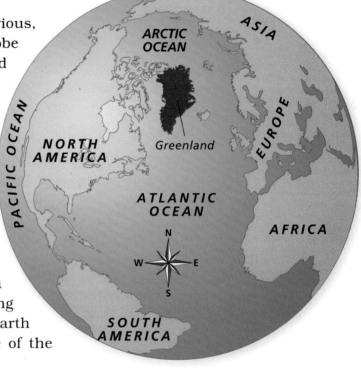

Globes are accurate, but for many uses maps are handier. Maps can show small areas in great detail. Because maps are flat, you can fold them and take them on a trip. Making a map, however, is like flattening an orange peel. When you take the round Earth and show it as a flat picture, the surface of the Earth gets distorted.

Let's compare how a globe and a map represent one part of the Earth. Look at the globe pictured above. You can see the continents of North America and South America. You can also see the large island called Greenland. On the globe, Greenland is very small compared to the rest of North America. On the globe Greenland is very small compared to North America.

Now look at how a map shows the same part of the world. This map is called a Mercator **projection**. A projection is a way of showing the round Earth on a flat map. There are many kinds of projections, often named for the person who invented them.

Find Greenland on both the map and the globe. On Earth, Africa is fourteen times bigger than Greenland. On Mercator's map, however, Greenland looks about the same size as Africa. The farther you go from the Equator (the imaginary line running around the middle of the Earth,) the more the Mercator projection distorts the size of places on the Earth.

Other projections distort the Earth less than Mercator's map. Look at the Robinson projection. On this map, Greenland looks much more like it does on the globe. Look at the Goode projection, which also has much less distortion than the Mercator projection. To reduce distortion, Goode's map leaves out parts of the oceans.

Goode's projection does a better job than Mercator's map in showing the true shapes and sizes of the Earth's land masses, but if you want to navigate a ship, don't use Goode's map or you'll sail off course!

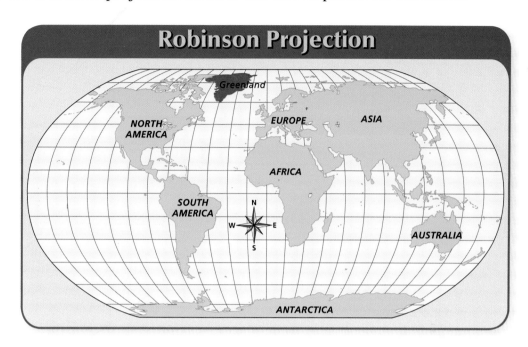

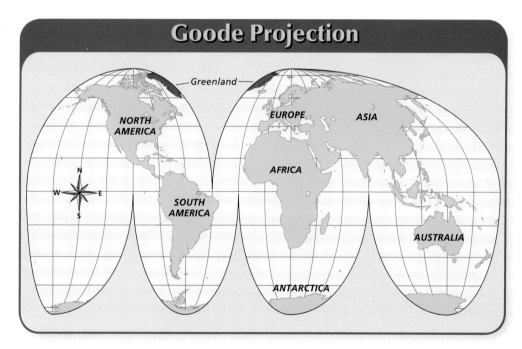

1. Review the seven continents. Find North America, South America, Europe, Africa, Asia, Australia, and Antarctica on a globe and on each of the maps.

2. Compare the Mercator projection to a globe. Besides Greenland, what other land masses are most distorted on the Mercator projection? (Look mostly near the North and South Poles.)

3. Compare the way North America looks on a globe to the way it looks on the Robinson and Goode projections. What differences do you see?

Look at the map of New York State. This map shows a much smaller area than a world map shows. Maps that show small areas have almost no distortion compared to maps that show the whole Earth.

A **map key**, also called a legend, helps you understand what is shown on the map. The key for this map is in the upper left corner. It tells you what symbols you can expect to find on the map and what those symbols mean.

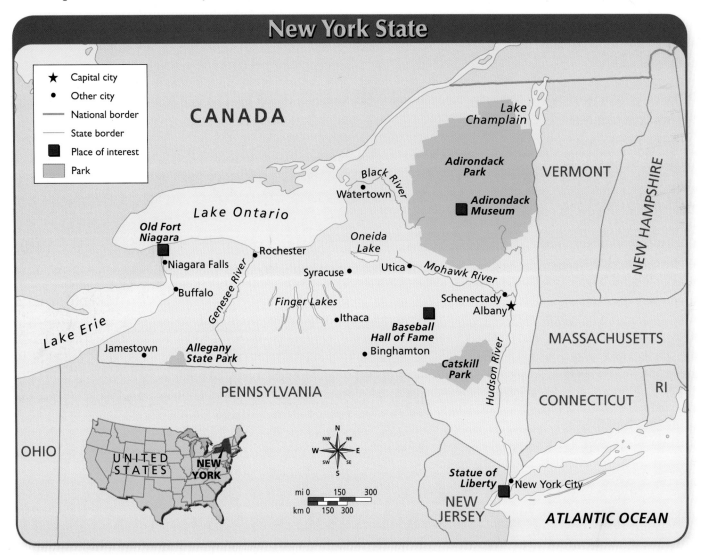

Use the map key to find these places:

4. Which city is the state capital of New York?

5. Identify two places of interest.

6. Identify two parks.

7. Identify two lakes.

This map has a **compass rose** to show the directions. As on many (but not all) maps, the compass rose shows north pointing toward the top of the map.

This compass rose shows the four **cardinal directions**: north, south, east, and west. It also shows the four **intermediate directions**: northeast, northwest, southeast, and southwest.

6

8. What direction would you travel to go from Buffalo to Schenectady?

9. What direction would you travel to go from New York City to Albany?

10. What direction would you travel to go from Utica to Jamestown?

11. Is Niagara Falls in the eastern or western part of the state?

12. Is New York City in the northwestern or southeastern part of the state?

13. Identify three states that touch the eastern border of New York. (A border is the dividing line between two places.)

14. Look at the small map of the United States in the bottom left corner, called a locator map. Is New York located in the northwestern or northeastern part of the country?

New York City

Skill Builder

Review

1. Which is a more accurate picture of the Earth, a map or a globe? Why?

2. Which shows more distortion, a Mercator projection or a Robinson projection?

3. Imagine you have two maps, each the same size as this book. One map shows the world. The other map shows the state of Texas. Which map shows more distortion?

4. Draw a compass rose. Label the cardinal and intermediate directions.

Try It Yourself

Fold a blank piece of paper in half and then in half the other way. Unfold the paper and turn it so a long side is on the bottom. Draw a light pencil line over each fold. Label one fold as the prime meridian and the other as the Equator. Draw the seven continents from memory. Rough shapes are good enough. Label the continents and the oceans. Check your work against the world map on pages 64-65.

Key Words: latitude, Equator, longitude, meridians, prime meridian, coordinate system, coordinates, absolute location, hemispheres

On many maps and globes, you can see crisscrossing lines with numbers by them. These lines and numbers form a grid system that allows us to describe the exact location of any place on Earth.

The lines running east to west around the Earth are lines of **latitude**, also called *parallels* (because parallel lines do not touch each other). These lines use units of measure called degrees to measure the distance north or south of the **Equator**, which is 0° latitude. (The symbol ° stands for degrees.) The 30th parallel north is the same as 30° N (north) latitude.

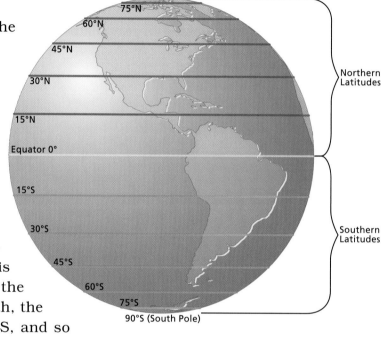

Look at the globe on the right. Locate the Equator at 0 degrees (0°). On this globe, the next line of latitude south of the equator is 15° S (south). Still going south, the next line of latitude is 30° S, then 45° S, and so on. The farthest south you can go is the South Pole, at latitude 90° S. The farthest north you can go is the North Pole, at latitude 90° N.

On a map or a globe the lines running north to south, from pole to pole are lines of **longitude**, also called *meridians*. Lines of longitude measure the distance east or west of the **prime meridian**, which is 0° longitude.

Look at the globe on the left. Find the prime meridian. On this globe, the first line of longitude east of the prime meridian is 15° E (east). The first line of longitude west of the prime meridian is 15° W (west). Unlike lines of latitude, lines of longitude eventually touch each other. Notice how the lines of longitude on the globe come together at the North Pole and the South Pole. At each of the poles, longitude equals 0°.

Together, lines of latitude and longitude form a grid system called the **coordinate system**. The latitude and longitude of a place make up the **coordinates** of that place. For example, on the world map below, the coordinates of the city of Cairo (in Africa) are 30° N, 31° E. When you state the coordinates of a place, you are describing its **absolute location**—its exact location on Earth. The absolute location of the city of New Orleans (in North America) is 30° N, 90° W.

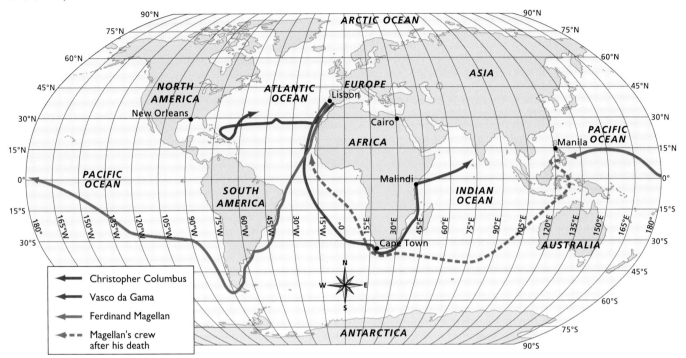

When Columbus set sail from Spain in 1492, he did not know there were continents to the west between Europe and Asia. But he and the other explorers of his time did know the world was round, and they knew how to measure latitude. Latitude measurements told them how far north or south they had gone from where they started. Without those calculations, their risky journeys would have been even more dangerous.

The map above shows the routes of three historic explorers. Notice that the farthest east or west you can go is 180°; in fact, 180° east and 180° west are the same line. This line of longitude cuts through the Pacific Ocean.

1. About how far south in latitude did Magellan go?

2. Who went farther south, Columbus or da Gama? About how far south in latitude did each explorer travel?

3. Which city along da Gama's route has an absolute location of 3° S, 40° E, Cape Town or Malindi?

4. Which city along Magellan's route has an absolute location of 38° N, 9° W, Manila or Lisbon?

A replica of the Niña, one of Columbus's ships

Hemispheres

You remember that the Equator is 0° latitude, while the prime meridian is 0° longitude. The Equator and prime meridian divide the Earth into **hemispheres**. The prefix *hemi* comes from the Greek word for "half," and a sphere, as you know, is a round object, like a globe.

The equator divides the globe into the Northern and Southern Hemispheres. The prime meridian divides the globe into the Eastern and Western Hemispheres. All places east of the prime meridian and west of the 180° longitude line are in the Eastern Hemisphere. All places west of the prime meridian and east of 180° are in the Western Hemisphere.

Every place on earth is in two hemispheres at once—either northern or southern, and either eastern or western. A large area such as a continent can span across many hemispheres. For example, as as you can see below, Africa is in both the Northern and Southern Hemispheres. And, while most of Africa is in the Eastern Hemisphere, part of the continent is in the Western Hemisphere as well. So, Africa is in all four hemispheres.

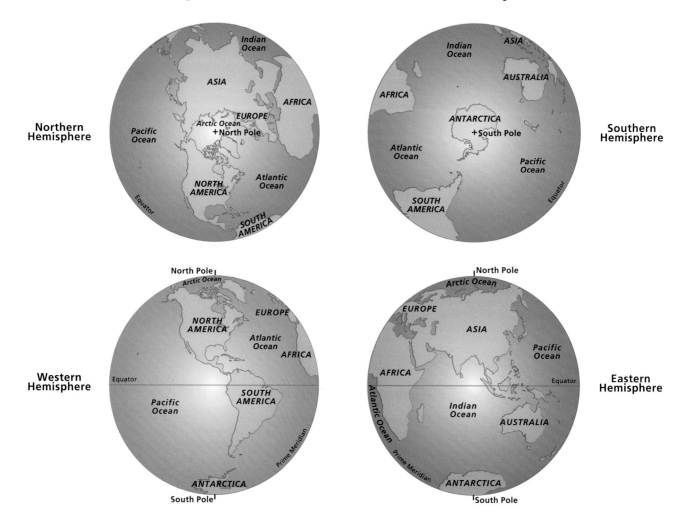

Look at these pictures of the Earth's four hemispheres.

5. Which continents are in both the Northern and the Southern Hemispheres?

6. Which ocean is only in the Northern Hemisphere?

7. Is South America in the Eastern or the Western Hemisphere?

8. Which continents are located in the Northern and Eastern Hemispheres?

Use the map of Georgia to answer the following questions about latitude and longitude.

9. Which city is near 33° N, 84° W, Macon or Albany?

10. Which city is near 31° N, 83° W, Brunswick or Valdosta?

11. Is the absolute location of Atlanta closer to 34° N, 84° W, or 33° N, 83° W?

12. What is the absolute location of Savannah?

13. About how far north and south does Georgia extend? Answer in degrees of latitude.

14. About how far east and west does Georgia extend? Answer in degrees of longitude.

15. Name two cities in Georgia located on the same line of longitude.

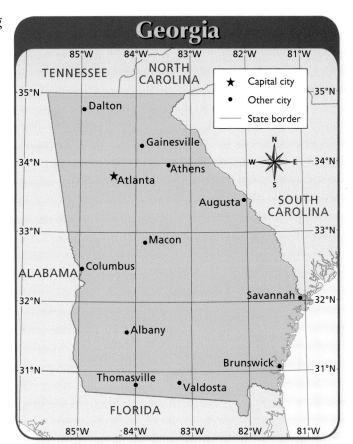

Skill Builder

Review

Use the map on page 9 to answer the following questions.

1. True or False: Lines of latitude measure distance north or south of the Equator.

2. True or False: Lines of longitude measure distance east or west of the prime meridian.

3. Lines of latitude are also called _____. Lines of longitude are also called _____.

4. In which two hemispheres is most of Asia located? In which two hemispheres is most of North America located?

5. If you are standing at 51° N, 101° E, in which two hemispheres are you located?

6. What is the absolute location of Cairo?

7. What is another name for the 0° line of latitude? What is another name for the 0° line of longitude?

8. On what continent would you find 38° N, 85° E?

9. On what continent would you find 10° S, 72° W?

10. On what continent would you find 28° S, 142° E?

Try It Yourself

Use the United States political map on pages 70-71 for the following activity.

A geography challenge: Give only the coordinates—the latitude and longitude—of one city on the map; ask a friend or parent to look at the map and identify the city. For example, you might ask, "What city is at 40° N, 75° W?"

Activity 3 Climate

Key Words: climate, precipitation, elevation, climograph

If you were traveling to Colorado in January, you would need to pack very warm clothes. If you were going to southern Florida, you might pack shorts and sandals for walking on the beach. Colorado and Florida are in the same country, but have different **climates**.

A beach in Florida where the climate is warm

Climate is the usual pattern of weather in a place over a very long period of time. While the weather can change quickly, from day to day or even from hour to hour, climate stays pretty much the same from year to year. The climate of a place can change, but from one year to the next, in any given season, you can expect similar patterns of temperature and **precipitation** (the moisture that falls as rain, snow, hail, or sleet). For example, the southeastern United States winter might bring days of cold weather or even snow, but the winters there are mild compared to those of the northeastern states.

Many factors determine climate. In general, the closer you are to the Equator, the warmer the climate. But climate is also affected by air currents, ocean currents, and **elevation**. Elevation, also called altitude, is the height of the land above sea level. A higher elevation usually means a cooler climate. For example, in the land now called Peru, Incas escaped the summer heat and humidity of their capital city, located in a valley, by moving higher into the mountains called the Andes, where the air is cool.

The ruins of the Inca city of Macchu Pichu, high in the Andes

This map shows the climate zones of the United States. All places in the same climate zone have similar patterns of precipitation and temperature. The map key describes the climate zones in the United States.

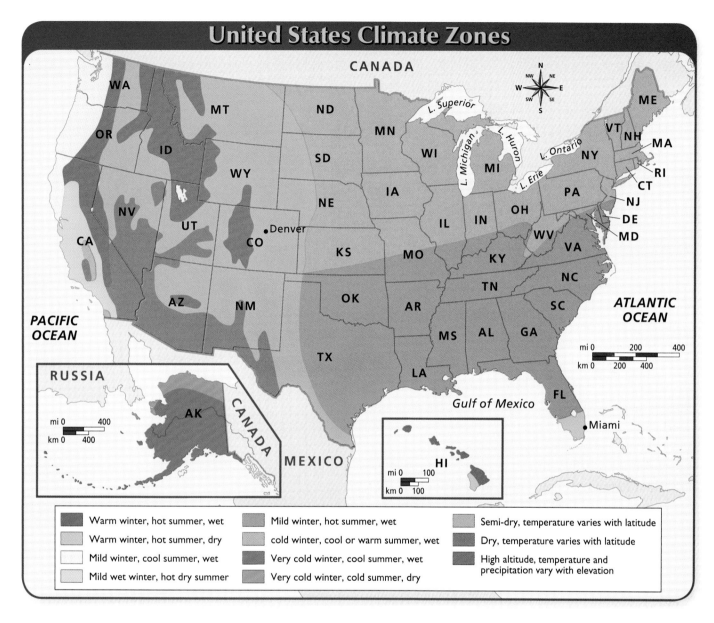

United States Climate Zones

Refer to the climate zones map to answer the following questions. If you need to, check the state abbreviation chart on page 72 to remind you of the names of the states.

1. In what climate zone or zones is your state located?

2. Which part of the country has a generally drier climate, the east or the west?

3. In what climate zone is Lake Michigan located? Are the summers there hot or cool?

4. In the mountains, the weather in high altitude areas is colder than in places at low elevations. Name five states with areas in the high altitude climate zone.

5. Are the summers wet or dry on the coast of northern California and Oregon?

6. Name three states with a dry, desert climate.

Using a Climograph

If you're planning a trip to Denver, Colorado, in January, you probably want to know how much precipitation usually falls there, and what kind of temperatures to expect in that month. To find out, you could use a **climograph** of the city.

A climograph usually shows the average temperature and precipitation in a certain place during a year. Look at the climographs below. The red lines show temperature while the blue bars show precipitation. The months are listed across the bottom of the climograph.

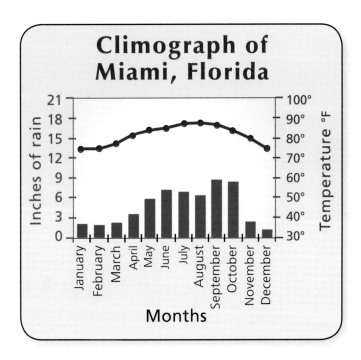

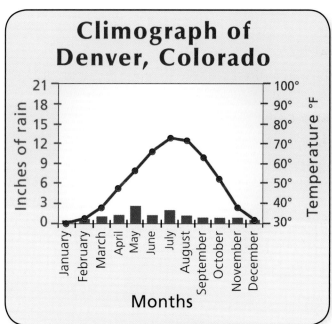

Look at the climographs of Miami and Denver above and answer the following questions.

7. Which city is in a drier climate, Denver or Miami?

8. In which month does Miami get the least amount of rain?

9. Which city has the steadiest temperatures throughout the year?

10. In which city would you need clothing for both cold and warm temperatures?

Adapting to Different Climates

People adapt to the climate where they live. You can see this, for example, in the different kinds of homes built by different Native American peoples in various regions.

In the hot and humid climate of Florida, the Seminoles built houses called chickees. One type of chickee had a raised platform for sleeping off the ground. There were no walls, so air could flow freely through the dwelling.

The Iroquois of the Northeast built homes called longhouses. In each longhouse there were several fireplaces to keep the people warm in the cold winters. The roofs of the longhouses were rounded to make the snow fall off instead of piling up.

An Iroquois longhouse

In the Southwest, the Anasazi people built homes called pueblos. The Anasazi are the ancestors of today's Pueblo Indians. These mud and straw homes kept the people cool in the summer and warm in the winter. Because this area gets little rain, the mud did not wash away.

A traditional pueblo

Skill Builder

Review

1. Explain the difference between climate and weather.

2. Look at the map on page 13. What part of the country has hotter summers, the southeast or the northeast?

3. On the map on page 13, find Miami, Florida, and Denver, Colorado. In what kind of climate zone is each city located?

4. How would you expect people who live in Idaho to adapt to their climate compared with people living in Hawaii?

Try It Yourself

On the map on page 13, locate the climate zone you live in. Describe the climate where you live. What are the general patterns of temperature and precipitation in the different seasons?

Map Scales

Key words: large scale, small scale

Imagine you're visiting the state of Tennessee. You have two maps, one like the map below, the other like the map on the next page. While both maps will help you plan your trip, they show very different things. One map shows the whole state. The other shows the city of Memphis, the largest city in the state.

These maps have different scales. Find the scale on both maps, at the bottom of each map. The scale lets you compare the distance on the map to the real distance on Earth. On the map of Tennessee, 1 inch equals 75 miles. On the map of Memphis, 1 inch equals 2 miles. You can measure the distance between two places on the map, and then use the map's scale to figure out how far apart these places really are on Earth.

On the map of Tennessee, the cities of Memphis and Dyersburg are 1 inch apart. You know that on this map 1 inch equals 75 miles. About how many miles is it from Memphis to Dyersburg?

Sometimes you will need to estimate. For example, on the map of Memphis, Libertyland is about 2 1/2 inches from the Memphis International Airport. How many miles does that represent? You know that 1 inch equals 2 miles on this map. So, 2 inches equals 4 miles. And 1/2 inch equals 1 mile. Add it all up. It's about 5 miles from Libertyland to the airport.

Use the scale on the map of Tennessee to answer these questions.

1. About how many miles is it from the capital city of Nashville to Knoxville?

2. People in the United States usually measure long distances in miles, while people in much of the rest of the world use kilometers (km). One mile is longer than one kilometer. About how many kilometers is it from Nashville to Knoxville?

Different maps show areas of different sizes. **Large scale** maps show small areas on Earth. The map of Memphis is a large scale map. Large scale maps often show details like streets or buildings. In contrast, the map of Tennessee is a **small scale** map. It does not show as much detail as the map of Memphis.

Compared to the map of Tennessee, a world map in this book has an even smaller scale. World maps can show entire continents and oceans in just a few inches. Remember this backward rule: small scale maps show large areas, while large scale maps show small areas.

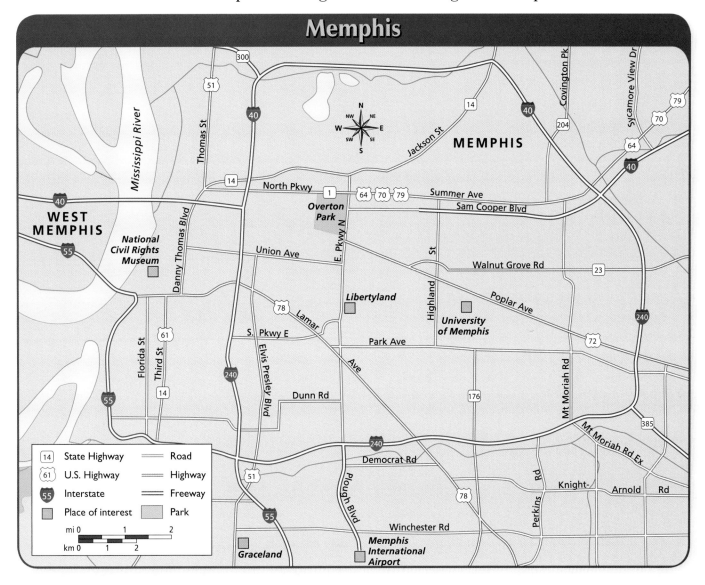

Practice figuring out distances in the real world by using the scale on the map of Memphis above. Then answer the questions below.

3. How far in miles is it from the National Civil Rights Museum to the University of Tennessee, Memphis?

4. How far in miles is it from Libertyland to Graceland, the home of the famous singer, Elvis Presley?

5. You are staying at a hotel near the University of Memphis. The hotel is at the intersection of Park Avenue and Highland Street. Use the map scale to calculate the distance along a straight line from your hotel to Graceland.

6. The distance in a straight line from one place to another is sometimes referred to as the distance "as the crow flies." A crow might be able to fly in a straight line from your hotel to Graceland. But if you drive, you have to use the roads. On the map, trace your finger along the roads that you would take to get from your hotel to Graceland. Which distance is farther, the straight line or the route you traced along the roads?

An Explorer's Routes

After Columbus's first voyage to North America in 1492, many European countries sent explorers across the Atlantic Ocean to explore this "new world." At that time, Europeans wanted to find a way to sail to Asia by going west. Such a route would allow easier access to Asia's valuable silk and spices.

An Italian explorer, Giovanni da Verrazzano, was hired by the king of France to explore the coast of North America. Verrazzano set sail in 1524. He traveled to an area along the North American coast that is now part of the state of North Carolina.

7. Refer to the world map on pages 66-67 to estimate the distance that Verrazzano traveled across the Atlantic Ocean. Use the map scale to help you calculate the distance from western France to the coast of North Carolina.

Giovanni da Verrazzano

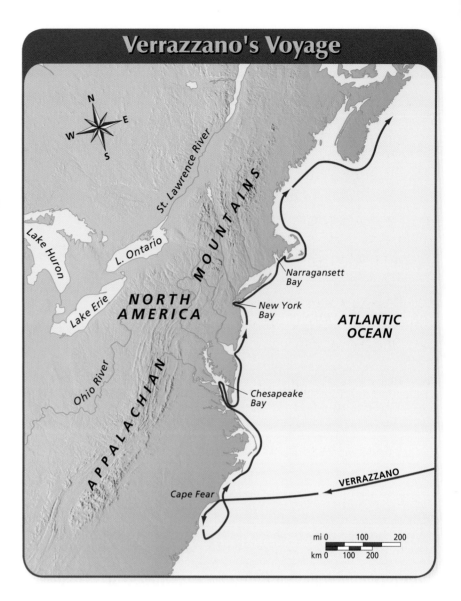

Verrazzano's Voyage

The map on this page shows Verrazzano's route along the coast of North America. The larger scale map on the following page shows only part of Verrazzano's route up the northeast coast. The route has been simplified to make it easier to estimate the distances he traveled.

Verrazzano believed that North America was a narrow strip of land. He hoped to find a shortcut across this land that would allow him to sail through to the Pacific Ocean. But, as we now know, there is no quick passage across North America to Asia.

Verrazzano first stopped at Cape Fear. From there he sailed north, looking for a way to sail through to Asia. He discovered a body of water that he thought led to the Pacific Ocean. Today we know that Verrazzano entered the Chesapeake Bay. Verrazzano explored parts of the Chesapeake Bay before continuing to sail north to what is now New York Bay. Today the Verrazzano-Narrows Bridge, named for the explorer spans the mouth of this bay.

Look at the map on the right to answer the following questions.

8. Use the map scale to calculate how far Verrazzano traveled between Cape Fear and the entrance to the Chesapeake Bay.

9. Use the map scale to calculate the distance from the Chesapeake Bay to New York Bay.

10. Use the map scale to calculate the distance from New York Bay to Narragansett Bay.

11. Add your calculations together to find the total distance Verrazzano traveled from Cape Fear to Narragansett Bay.

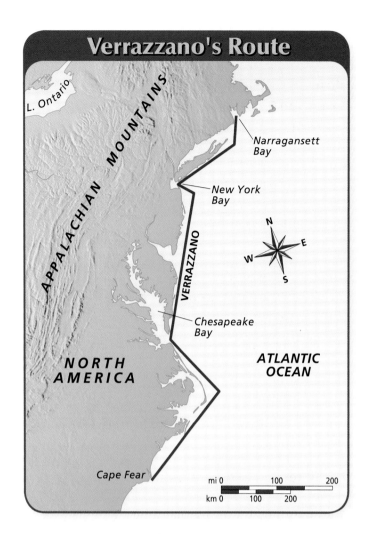

Skill Builder

Review

1. Imagine that you have three maps. The first shows the state of Florida. The second shows a neighborhood in Miami, a city in Florida. The third shows all the states on the East Coast. Which map has the largest scale? Which map has the smallest scale?

2. Use the map of the United States on pages 70-71 to estimate the distances between these cities:

   • Baltimore, Maryland, and Buffalo, New York

   • Kansas City, Missouri, and Albuquerque, New Mexico

   • Jackson, Mississippi, and San Diego, California

   • Carson City, Nevada, and Indianapolis, Indiana

Try It Yourself

Choose three cities in the United States. Imagine you are planning a trip to each of these cities. Measure the distance you will travel on your trip. Start at your hometown, go to each city, and return home again. How many miles is it from one city to the next? How many total miles will you travel?

Key Words: landform, mountain, mountain range, basin, peak, desert, island, peninsula, plateau, plain, relief map, elevation, piedmont, coastal plain, valley

You have probably sung about "purple *mountain* majesties upon the fruited *plain*." Mountains and plains are two kinds of **landforms**. Landforms are features of the Earth's surface. Major landforms include:

- **mountain:** the highest type of landform, higher than hills
- **mountain range:** a series of mountains that form a group
- **basin:** all the land drained by a river and by all the streams flowing into the river
- **peak:** a high mountain or the pointed top of a mountain
- **desert:** a dry, often sandy area that gets very little rain
- **island:** land that is completely surrounded by water
- **peninsula:** a body of land that is almost completely surrounded by water
- **plateau:** a large area of high, flat land
- **plain:** a large area of mostly flat land with few trees

The **relief map** on the opposite page shows the major landforms in the United States. A relief map shows the higher and lower parts of an area. To show **elevation**—the height of the land above sea level (the level of the ocean)—relief maps often use different colors and textures. For example, mountains on a relief map might look bumpy, while plains look smooth.

Elevation changes a lot from place to place in the United States. The highest point in the United States, Mount McKinley in Alaska, is 20,320 feet above sea level. The lowest point, Death Valley in California, has an elevation of 282 feet *below* sea level. The map on the next page uses colors to show different elevations in the United States. For example, the darker green areas are between 0 and 650 feet above sea level, while the darker orange areas are over 6,560 feet above sea level.

A mountain peak in the Cascade Range in Washington

A plain in the central United States

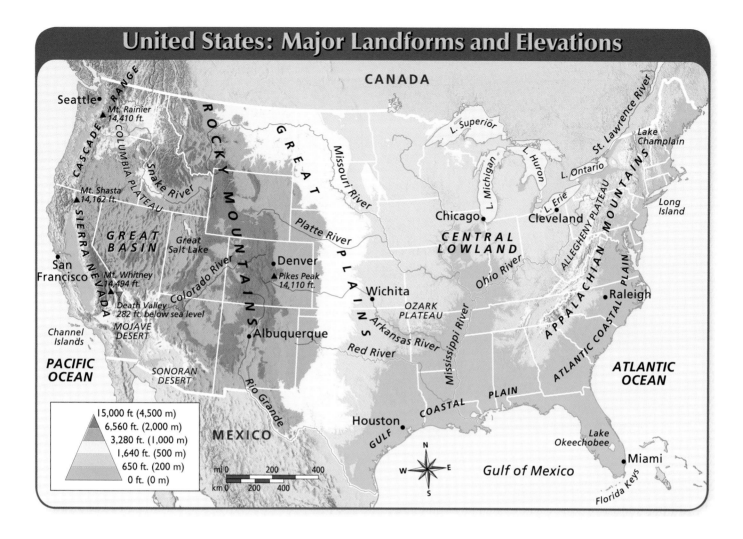

United States: Major Landforms and Elevations

1. What is the largest mountain range in the western United States? What is the largest mountain range in the eastern United States? Which mountain range is higher? How can you tell?

2. Find the Ozark Plateau and the Columbia Plateau on the map. Which is closer to sea level?

3. The highest and lowest elevations shown on this map are both in the west. Identify these places and their elevations.

4. Which city is at a higher elevation—Raleigh, North Carolina, or Denver, Colorado?

5. Is the elevation higher in the Great Plains or along the Atlantic Coastal Plain?

6. The Missouri River flows into the Mississippi River. In what mountains does the Missouri River begin?

7. Identify two other rivers that flow into the Mississippi River.

8. Which southeastern state is mostly a large peninsula? What bodies of water surround this peninsula?

9. What type of landform are the Florida Keys?

10. Do most mountain ranges in the United States run north-south or east-west?

11. Which part of the United States has the most deserts—western, central, or eastern?

12. The Great Basin is not as flat as the Great Plains. How is this shown on the map?

The map below shows the state of Virginia. The map uses colors to indicate the major landforms in different parts of the state.

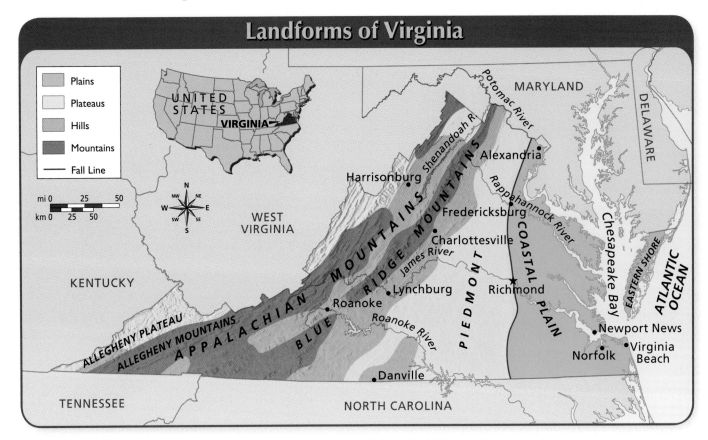

Study these terms and then use the map above to answer the questions below.

- **piedmont:** an area of land at the foot of a mountain range

- **coastal plain:** low, flat land near the ocean

- **valley:** a low area between mountains or hills

13. The Allegheny Mountains and the Blue Ridge Mountains are both parts of a larger mountain chain. What is this larger mountain chain called?

14. The Piedmont region of Virginia extends from the foot of the Blue Ridge Mountains to the Coastal Plain. The land of the Piedmont is higher than the land of the Coastal Plain. What kind of landform is the Piedmont?

15. The Shenandoah River runs through a valley called the Shenandoah Valley. Which mountains lie just to the east of this valley?

16. The Eastern Shore of Virginia is almost entirely surrounded by water, with the Chesapeake Bay to the west and the Atlantic Ocean to the east. What kind of landform is the Eastern Shore?

17. If you traveled from Newport News to Charlottesville, would you go from higher to lower elevation, or from lower to higher?

18. Into what body of water do the James and Rappahannock Rivers flow?

On the map on the opposite page, find the city of Alexandria, Virginia, one of the oldest cities in the United States. Before the American Revolution, Alexandria was a busy port. Farmers to the north and west brought their tobacco to Alexandria to load on ships going to England. Look again at the map. You will see that Alexandria is on the Potomac River. Why did ships stop at Alexandria instead of going farther inland up the Potomac?

A town in the Coastal Plain of Virginia

The answer to that question shows us how landforms affect human activity and history. Locate the Fall Line on the map. Virginia's Coastal Plain and the Piedmont meet at this line of small waterfalls and rapids (places in rivers where the water runs swiftly and roughly). The land to the west of the Fall Line is hard and rocky. The land to the east is softer. As Virginia's rivers flow eastward from the Piedmont to the Coastal Plain, when they cross from the hard rock to the softer land, they create waterfalls. That's why the ships stopped at Alexandria!

The Great Falls of the Potomac River

19. Name two cities in Virginia south of Alexandria that are located on rivers where the Coastal Plain and the Piedmont meet. On what rivers are these cities located?

Skill Builder

Review

1. What does a relief map show?

2. Name four major landforms found in the United States.

3. In which landform region would you find more farming—mountains or plains?

4. On which coast is there a larger coastal plain—the Atlantic coast or the Pacific coast?

5. Name two cities at elevations over 3,300 feet.

6. In colonial times, as settlers began to move westward, what large mountain range slowed their progress?

Try It Yourself

What types of landforms can you see near your home? What other types of landforms are found in your state? How far would you have to travel to reach the nearest mountains? To reach sea level?

Bodies of Water

Key Words: lake, river, source, mouth, tributary, gulf, bay, estuary, harbor

Long ago, the first civilizations began along rivers. Early traders sailed on the seas. Explorers set out in ships and crossed vast oceans.

Rivers, seas, oceans—these bodies of water have shaped the course of history. Three-fourths of the Earth's surface is covered by water. Much of this water is the salt water that makes up the Earth's four oceans and many seas.

Chesapeake Bay

1. Look at the world map on pages 64-65. Locate the Earth's four oceans: Atlantic, Pacific, Indian, and Arctic.

2. Which ocean borders the west coast of the United States? Which borders the east coast?

Review the terms below, and then refer to the map on pages 68-69 to answer the questions:

- **lake:** a body of water surrounded by land on all sides; lakes usually hold freshwater
- **river:** a large freshwater stream that flows over land
- **source:** the beginning of a river
- **mouth:** the place where a river flows into another body of water, such as a lake, a larger river, or the ocean
- **tributary:** a river that flows into another river
- **gulf:** a part of a sea or ocean that extends into the land; usually larger than a bay
- **bay:** a small body of water partly surrounded by land; usually smaller than a gulf
- **estuary:** a partly enclosed body of water where fresh river water mixes with salt water from the ocean

3. Locate the five Great Lakes: Superior, Michigan, Huron, Erie, and Ontario

4. Locate the nation's largest estuary, the Chesapeake Bay.

5. The Missouri River has its source in the Rocky Mountains. What body of water does it flow into?

6. The Rio Grande also begins in the Rockies. Where is this river's mouth?

7. Find the Arkansas River. This river is a tributary—it flows into another river. Name this other river.

8. List six states you would pass through if you traveled from north to south down the Mississippi River.

Most of the early explorers of North America traveled on oceans, lakes, or rivers. The map below shows the routes of some of these early explorers.

9. Name two explorers who traveled along the coasts of North America but did not go inland.

10. What body of water did Marquette and Joliet explore as they went south?

11. What bay on the map was named for the Englishman who explored it?

12. What explorer traveled down the Mississippi River and then into the Gulf of Mexico?

13. What major river did Coronado cross?

14. What explorer traveled part way down the St. Lawrence River?

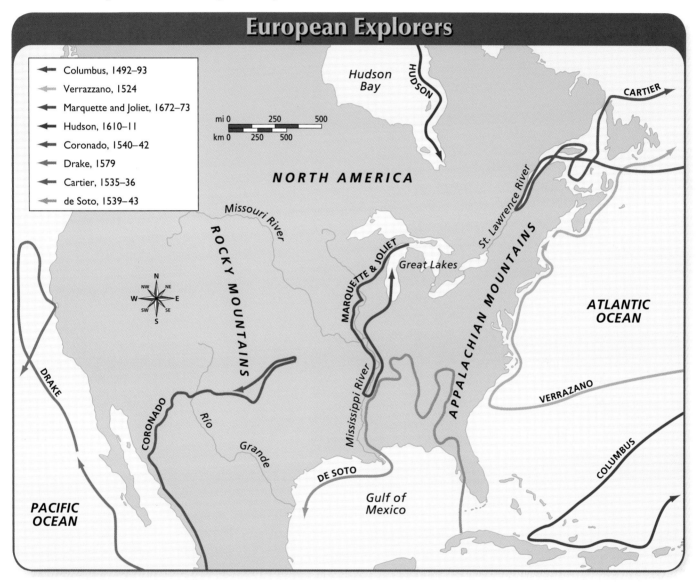

Settling Along Bodies of Water

As you study the past, you can see a clear pattern—towns and cities often developed near oceans, lakes, and rivers. Along the coast, sheltered areas called **harbors** provided calm waters where ships could dock to load and unload people and goods. Rivers provided freshwater and routes inland. Early trading centers grew where rivers flow into an ocean or gulf. Over time, many of these trading centers became large cities, such as New Orleans and Boston. In some areas, the strong flow of river water provided power for mills and early factories. Cities grew as people came to work in factories in places like Lowell, Massachusetts, and Pittsburgh, Pennsylvania.

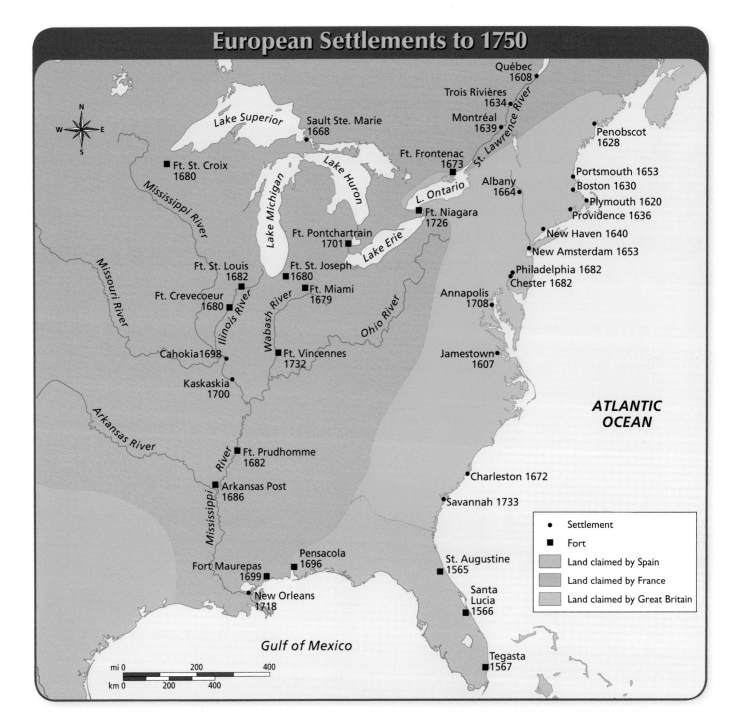

European Settlements to 1750

Besides Britain, both France and Spain sent people to explore along many of North America's rivers and lakes. The French established many settlements and forts. They often built their forts along rivers or on lake shores. With water on one side, the forts were easier to defend against attacks. Because traveling on rivers and lakes was often easier than traveling on land, these forts also became centers of trade.

The Spanish also built protected settlements. Many of the Spanish settlements were Catholic missions established to convert Indians to Christianity. Like the French forts, the Spanish missions were often built near rivers or harbors.

The map above shows some of the forts, missions, and other settlements in the eastern half of North America in colonial times. Use the map key and map to find out which European country claimed which parts of North America as of 1750.

Look at the map on the opposite page and answer the following questions.

15. On which river do you see the most settlements?

16. What lake was Fort St. Croix nearest to?

17. Name one French settlement on the St. Lawrence River.

18. What three lakes are within just a few miles of Sault Ste. Marie?

The fort at St. Augustine, Florida

19. Name one fort along the Wabash River.

20. Which settlement on the Mississippi River was established first?

21. What is the earliest Spanish settlement on the map?

22. Were the earliest settlements established on rivers or on the coast? Why?

Skill Builder

Review

1. Name the Earth's four oceans. Locate them on a globe or world map.

Use the United States physical map on pages 68-69 to help you answer the following questions.

2. Standing on the shore in California, you can see the _____ Ocean. Standing on the shore in Virginia, you can see the _____ Ocean.

3. Name two tributaries in the United States. Into what rivers do these tributaries flow?

4. The Mississippi River and the Rio Grande both flow into the same body of water. Name this body of water.

5. Identify and locate the five Great Lakes.

6. What river flows out of Lake Ontario?

7. Explain two reasons why towns and cities are often found near bodies of water.

Try It Yourself

Find the Tennessee River and the Ohio River on the United States physical map on pages 68-69. Is the source of each closer to the Mississippi River or to the Atlantic Ocean? Do these rivers flow into the Mississippi River or into the Atlantic Ocean? Can you figure out why the rivers do not flow into the closer of the two bodies of water?

Activity 7 Resources and Trade

Key Words: natural resources, animal, plant, mineral, fossil fuel, renewable resources, agriculture nonrenewable resources, exported, trade, raw materials, imported, triangular trade

An oil derrick pumping oil out of the ground

If you eat a breakfast of cereal or toast or eggs, you're using natural resources. If you wear a cotton tee shirt or leather shoes, you're using natural resources. If you ride in an automobile, you're using natural resources—lots of them.

Natural resources are materials we use that come from nature. Here are examples of different kinds of natural resources:

- **animal resources:** fish, cattle, pigs, and other animals we raise for food
- **plant resources:** trees or crops that we use for food and lumber
- **mineral resources:** metals such as copper or aluminum
- **fossil fuels:** oil and natural gas we use for fuel

Animals and plants are **renewable resources**—we can grow or raise more, though we still must be careful not to overuse them. On farms and ranches, people involved in **agriculture** grow crops and raise many kinds of animals. Agriculture is both a business and a science. Some people grow crops and raise livestock, such as cattle or sheep, to sell. Others study ways to improve agriculture, for example, by making crops resist diseases, or by raising cows that produce more milk.

Mineral resources and fossil fuels are **nonrenewable resources**—once we use them, we can't grow them or make more. If we cut down trees for lumber, we can plant more. But the Earth only has so much copper, aluminum, and other mineral resources. The supply of fossil fuels, such as oil and coal, is limited. If we are not careful, we can run out.

Stacks of lumber, made from trees

1. Give one example of each of these kinds of resources: animal, plant, mineral, and fossil fuel. Explain how we use each.

2. Explain the difference between renewable and nonrenewable resources, and give an example of each.

Natural Resources in Colonial Times

The map below shows some of the natural resources that people used in the 13 original British ííícolonies. Use the map key to help you answer the following questions.

Colonists used beaver and other animal furs and skins to make warm clothing.

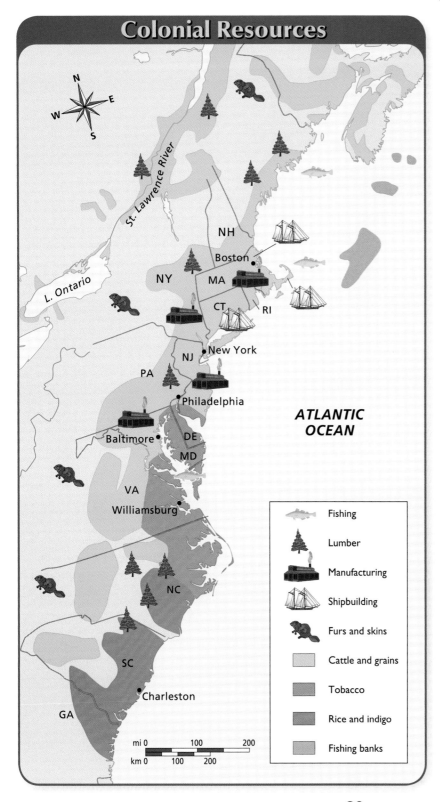

3. Building ships and manufacturing products such as tools or stoves are two types of industry. Which area of the 13 colonies had more industry, the North or the South?

4. In which colony was lumber more plentiful, North Carolina or Connecticut?

5. Indigo is a non-food crop used to make dark blue dye for cloth. Tobacco is another non-food plant. Were these crops mainly grown in the northern or southern colonies?

6. If you could visit Williamsburg in 1750, what crop would you be most likely to see on farms near the city?

7. Were furs and skins found mainly in the eastern or western regions of the colonies?

8. Was the business of fishing more common in the North or the South?

The colonists found themselves in a land rich with natural resources. They used some of these resources for everyday living—to build their homes, make their clothes, or provide their meals. They had more than they needed, so they **exported** many resources to England. To export is to send goods to another place. Resources such as lumber, indigo, and furs became part of the **trade** between the colonists and England. Trade is the business of buying and selling or exchanging goods.

The colonists exported **raw materials**—resources used to make other products—to England. From these raw materials, manufacturers in England made goods such as furniture and clothing. The colonists then **imported** these manufactured goods from England. To import is to bring goods in from another place. So, in their trade with England, the colonists exported raw materials and imported manufactured goods. You can see this trade between the colonies and England on the map. The arrows show the directions in which goods traveled.

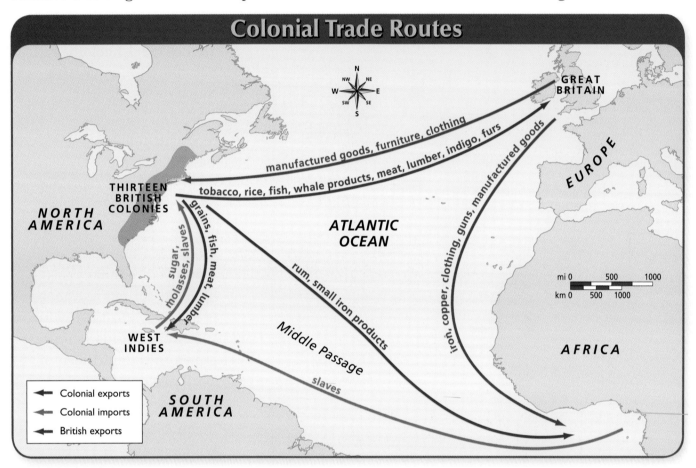

The Triangular Trade and Slavery

This map also shows trade between the colonies and the Caribbean and between the colonies and Africa. Part of this trading system was the terrible trade in people—the slave trade. The slave trade was part of a pattern of trade called the **triangular trade**. The three "sides" of this trade triangle went like this:

a. Ships carried simple manufactured goods from New England to the west coast of Africa. The merchants sold their goods and bought captured Africans from slave traders.

b. In the "Middle Passage," the merchants took their captives across the Atlantic to South America and to the islands of the West Indies. The ships were so crowded and filthy that many of the captives died on the journey.

c. After selling some slaves, merchants loaded their ships with sugar and molasses. Then they sailed back to the colonies where they sold the sugar, molasses, and the rest of the slaves.

Look at the map on the opposite page and answer the following questions.

9. Name two animal resources that the colonies exported to England.

10. Name three plant resources that the colonies exported.

11. Name two major exports from England to the colonies.

12. Name two resources that the Europeans exported to Africa.

13. Where did enslaved people stop before they reached Britain's North American colonies?

Wooden sailing ships transported goods across the Atlantic Ocean.

Skill Builder

Review

1. Is tobacco an animal, plant, or mineral resource?

2. Give an example of a fossil fuel. Are fossil fuels renewable or nonrenewable resources?

3. A colonial company sells wood to a company in England. From this wood, the English company makes furniture, which it exports to the colonies. In this trade, what is the raw material? What is the manufactured good?

4. What did the colonies mainly export to England, raw materials or manufactured goods?

5. Which was a common export from the Southern colonies, rice or iron tools?

6. What is the Middle Passage?

Try It Yourself

Think about the natural resources you use in your daily life. Most of your food comes from natural resources. Much of your clothing does, too. You might use cooking utensils made of copper or aluminum. You might use oil or natural gas to heat your home. Make a list of at least eight natural resources you use regularly. Categorize the resources you list as animal, plant, mineral, or fossil fuel.

Key Words: transportation map, canals, migration

In 1803, the French sold the United States a huge piece of land that stretched from the Mississippi River to the Rocky Mountains. The deal was known as the Louisiana Purchase. It doubled the size of the young United States.

President Thomas Jefferson asked Meriwether Lewis and William Clark to lead a small group of men to explore this new territory and beyond. He wanted them to travel by river as far as possible and find a way through the Rocky Mountains to the Pacific Ocean.

A **transportation map** can show the routes people follow to get from one place to another. Look at the map below. This map shows the route of two famous explorations in the early 1800s. Lewis and Clark went from St. Louis on the Mississippi River to the Pacific Ocean near what is now Portland, Oregon. Another explorer, Zebulon Pike, explored areas farther south, including lands then controlled by Spain

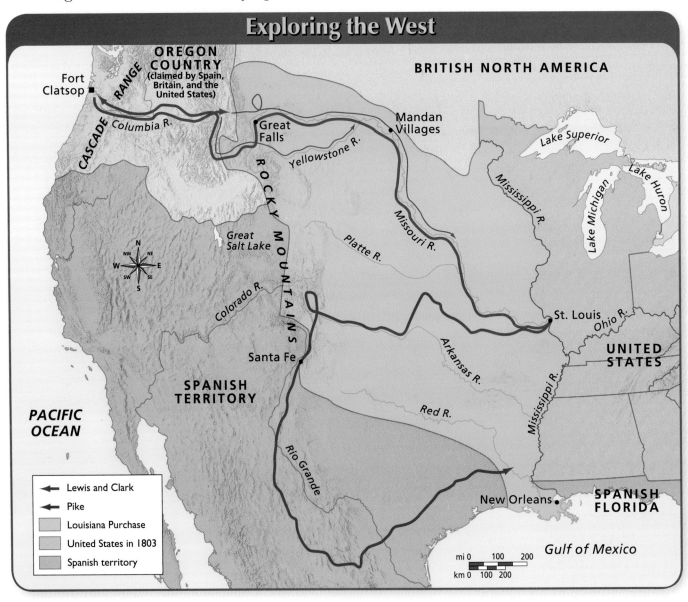

Exploring the West

Use the map of exploration on the opposite page to answer the questions.

1. Name three major rivers Lewis and Clark followed during their journey.

2. Name two mountain ranges Lewis and Clark crossed to reach the Pacific Ocean.

3. About how many miles did Lewis and Clark travel from St. Louis to the Pacific and back?

4. Zebulon Pike did not have permission to enter Spanish territory, but he did so anyway. At what city did he cross the border into Spanish territory?

5. Pike crossed a large river in Spanish territory twice. Name this river.

6. What physical feature might have forced Pike to turn south from the source of the Arkansas River?

Roads and Canals

By 1840, the eastern United States had many roads, as well as a number of man-made waterways called **canals**. These transportation routes opened the way for merchants to trade their goods and for more people than ever before to move west of the Appalachian Mountains.

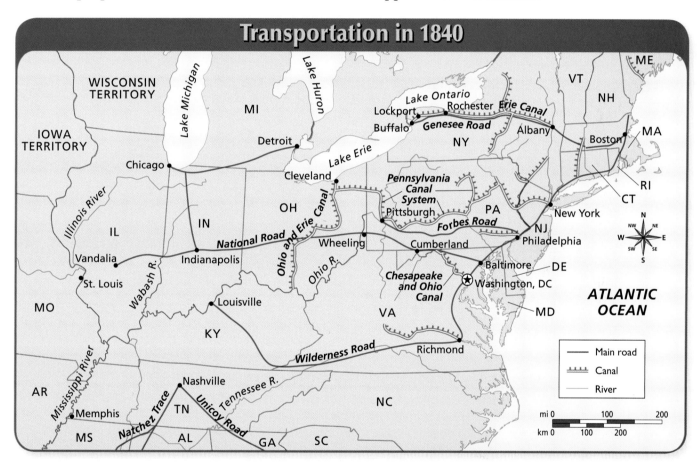

The transportation map above shows major roads and canals in the U.S. around 1840. The map also shows different means of transportation.

7. Name three canals in operation by 1840.

8. Name three primary roads being used in 1840.

9. If you wanted to get to St. Louis, Missouri, from Baltimore, Maryland, what primary road would you follow most of the way?

10. What two bodies of water does the Erie Canal connect?

11. Name three states where there were no primary roads and no major canals in 1840. What do you think might explain this?

Going West

Before the 1860s, pioneers who wanted to go west of the Mississippi River followed trails along older Indian paths. It might take six months to travel the 2,000 miles from Missouri to Oregon. In spite of the hardships, a great **migration** took place between 1840 and 1870. More than 350,000 people moved to the American West.

New routes and transportation methods eventually made the journey easier for the settlers. In 1869, the Central Pacific Railroad from the east and Union Pacific Railroad from the west were connected to complete the Transcontinental Railroad. For the first time, a major transportation route connected the country from coast to coast.

12. If it took six months (about 180 days) to travel 2,000 miles from Missouri to Oregon, how many miles did people cover in one day, on average? In what regions do you think they could go faster than the average, and where do you think they went slower? Why?

13. The Central Pacific and Union Pacific Railroads met at Promontory Point in the Utah Territory. What major city was located nearby?

14. About how far is it from one end of the Central Pacific Railroad to the other?

15. What three rivers did the Oregon Trail follow?

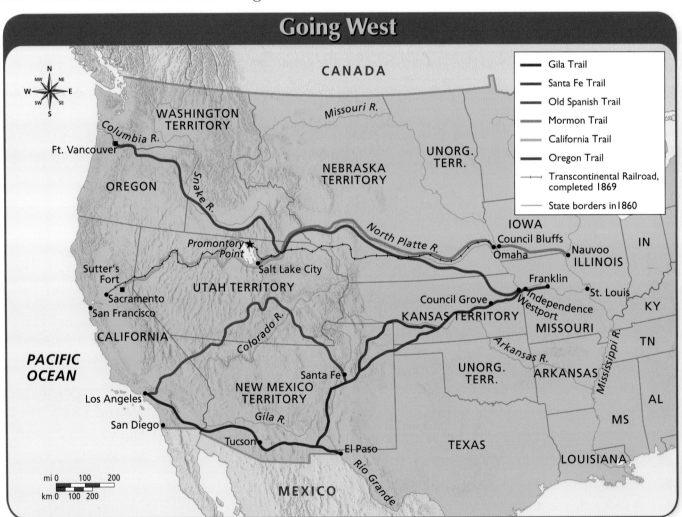

Riding Down the Highway

In the late 1800s, many Americans made long trips by train. Today, many more people drive on the interstate highways. Look at the map of the U.S. interstate highway system. Each highway has a number. You can see the numbers inside the blue and red interstate symbols.

16. What interstate would you use to drive from St. Louis, Missouri, to Denver, Colorado?

17. Name two western cities connected by Interstate 10.

18. If you drove from Albuquerque to Kansas City, which two interstates would you take?

19. Interstate 5 runs north-south along the west coast. Name three cities it passes through.

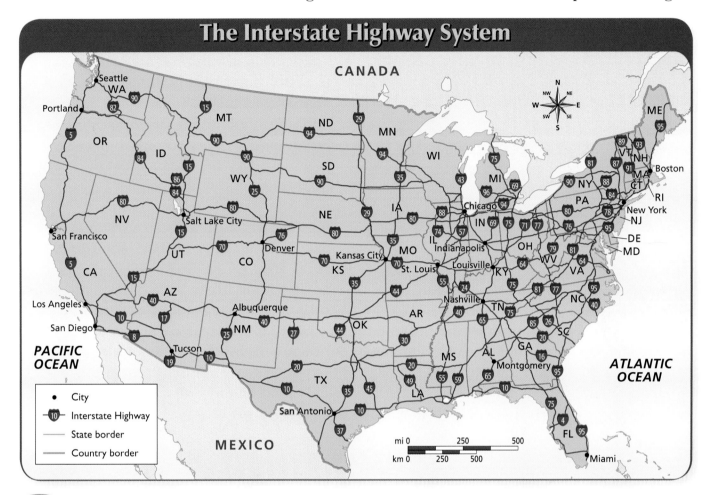

Skill Builder

Review

1. See the map on page 34. Which wagon trail went farther south, the Santa Fe or the Gila?

2. Compare the map on page 35 with the physical map on pages 68-69. What landform region separates Route 15 and Route 25?

3. In the early 1800s, very few people traveled from the eastern United States to the west coast. Name two changes in transportation that have made it easier for people to travel across the country.

Try It Yourself

Physical geography influences transportation routes. As people moved west across North America, they had to find routes through or around mountains, rivers, and deserts. If you were going west in the early 1800s, which of the trails shown on the map on page 34 would you follow? What challenges would you expect to meet on this route?

Key Words: urban, suburban, rural, suburbs, population, population density, megalopolis

San Francisco is a city, an urban area with a large, dense population.

Take a look around the area where you live. Do you see fields, forests, and lots of space? Do you see houses, apartments, and office buildings? Do you see many buildings? Are they far apart or packed together? Are the streets quiet or crowded with cars, buses, and people?

Another way to ask these questions is to ask if you live in an **urban**, **suburban**, or **rural** area. Cities are considered urban areas. Urban areas have large populations with people living close together. In the center of an urban area you often see tall buildings called skyscrapers, where many people work. Some of these people might go home to apartments in the city. Many of them make a longer trip to communities around the edge of the city, called **suburbs**. Most suburban areas have businesses, parks, shopping centers, and many houses with yards. People in suburbs usually work either in the community or in the nearby city.

In the United States today, most people live in urban or suburban areas. A hundred years ago, that was not true. Back then most people lived in rural areas. Rural areas include the countryside, with farms, forests, small towns, and villages.

Population Density Maps

The **population** is the total number of people living in an area. **Population density** is the term that describes the average number of people living in an area of a certain size. We often state population density in terms of the *average number of people per square mile*—that is, how many people are living in a square whose sides are each one mile long. In 2000, the city of Chicago had a population density of more than 12,000 people per square mile. In the

Many people live in the suburban areas near a city.

same year, about 100 miles southwest of Chicago, Bureau County had a population density of less than 50 people per square mile. In urban areas like Chicago, where a lot of people live close together, the population density is *high*. In rural areas like Bureau County, where people live far apart, the population density is *low*.

The map below shows population density in the United States in the year 2000. Use the map and the map key to answer the following questions.

1. Which color on the map shows the highest population density? Which color shows the lowest population density?

2. Was the population density of the state of Massachusetts 45-90 per square mile, or 90 or more?

3. Which area of the United States has the higher population density, the northeast or the northwest?

Rural farm areas are less populated than suburban areas.

4. Which state has a higher population density, New Jersey or Maine?

5. Which state has a higher population density, Wyoming or Illinois?

6. When the United States was first settled, most people lived near a body of water (such as a lake, river, or ocean). Looking at the map below, would you say this is still true today?

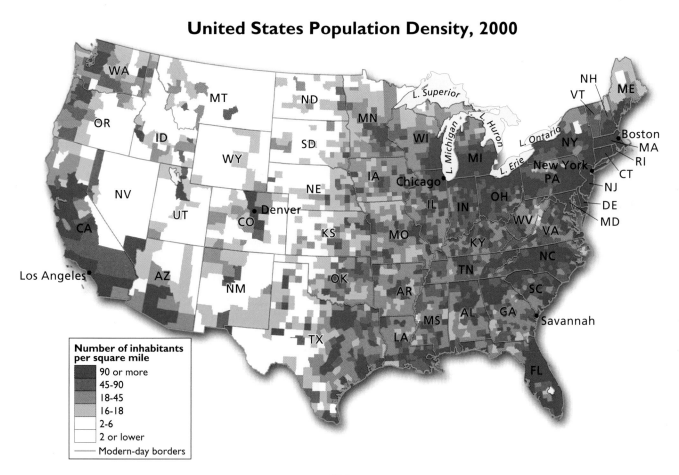

United States Population Density, 2000

Population Change Over Time

Population density maps can show the change in population in an area over time. Compare the two maps below. The top map shows the population density of the United States in the year 1790, when the country's western border was the Mississippi River. The bottom map shows the population density of the United States in 1870. Notice that in 1790 there were no purple areas, because at that time even the largest cities did not have more than 90 people per square mile.

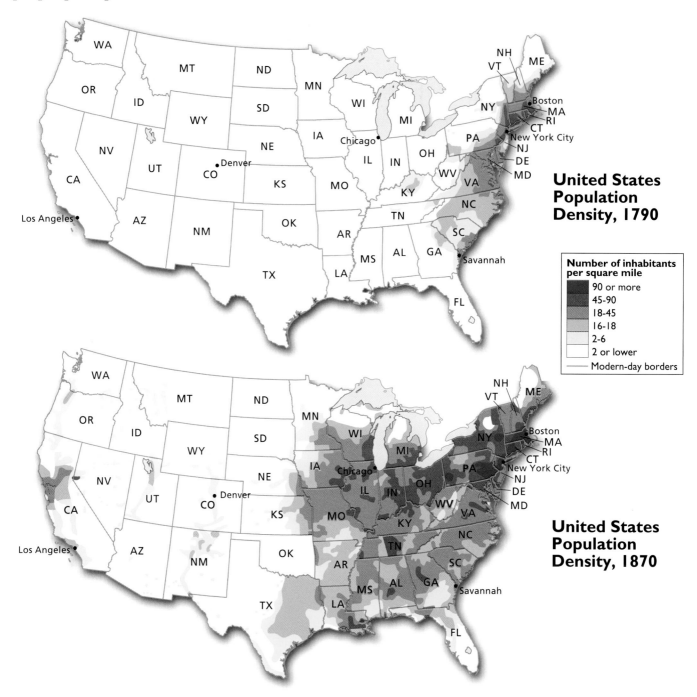

United States Population Density, 1790

United States Population Density, 1870

Number of inhabitants per square mile
- 90 or more
- 45-90
- 18-45
- 16-18
- 2-6
- 2 or lower
- Modern-day borders

7. Which area of the country had the highest population density in 1790? In 1870?

8. In 1790, no areas west of the Mississippi River had population densities over two people per square mile. By 1870, which western states had the biggest increase in population density?

9. Which state had a higher population density in 1790, South Carolina or Connecticut?

10. Name two states that had areas with the highest population density in 1870.

Bright City Lights

Have you ever seen a city at night? At night, urban areas have many more lights than rural areas. Look at the satellite photo below. It shows the lights of the United States at night. On the map, the most densely populated areas are the most brightly lit.

In some areas you can see patches of white joined together. These "strings" of light occur when the populations of several cities spread out toward each other. A densely populated region made up of several cities and the area around them is called a **megalopolis** (meh-guh-LAH-puh-lus), a term that comes from Greek words meaning "very large city."

A satellite image of the United States at night

Use the United States map on pages 70-71 to locate the places named in the following questions.

11. Which areas of Florida have the higher population density, the coasts or the interior?

12. Los Angeles and San Diego form the largest megalopolis in the western United States. Find this area on the satellite photo.

13. The largest megalopolis in the country includes five major eastern cities: Boston, New York, Philadelphia, Baltimore, and Washington, D.C. Find this megalopolis on the satellite image.

Skill Builder

Review

1. In 1790, which urban area had a higher population density, Boston or Savannah?

2. In 1870, which urban area had a higher population density, Los Angeles or New York?

3. Is population density generally higher close to water or farther away from water?

4. Compare the map of population density in 2000 with the physical map of the United States on pages 68-69. Can you explain why there are so few people per square mile in central Nevada?

Try It Yourself

Find your state on the U.S. population density maps for 1870 and 2000. Describe how its population density changed between 1870 and 2000.

Key Words: historical map, levee

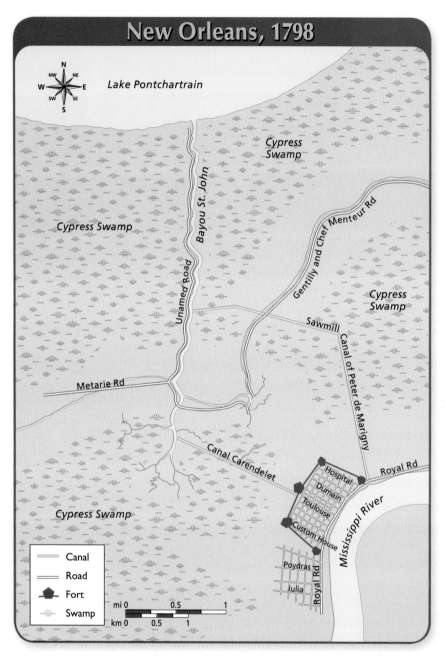

New Orleans, 1798

Map labels: Lake Pontchartrain · Cypress Swamp · Bayou St. John · Gentilly and Chef Menteur Rd · Unamed Road · Sawmill · Canal of Peter de Marigny · Metarie Rd · Canal Carendelet · Cypress Swamp · Hospital · Dumain · Toulouse · Custom House · Royal Rd · Poydras · Julia · Royal Rd · Mississippi River

Legend: Canal · Road · Fort · Swamp · mi 0 · 0.5 · 1 · km 0 · 0.5 · 1

In 1718, a French explorer, Jean-Baptiste de Bienville, founded a city on the banks of the Mississippi River, in what is now part of southeastern Louisiana. He named the city *New Orleans* in honor of France's ruler, Philippe d'Orléans.

For the site of the new city, Bienville chose the highest ground in the area on a great bend in the Mississippi River. This high ground was safer and healthier than the swampy, disease-ridden lowland nearby, which often flooded from the Mississippi River and from Lake Pontchartrain just to the north.

Bienville chose an excellent location for trade. French traders and fur trappers had lived in the area for several years. Native Americans traded there, too. The river was the major trade route to the north, and the city was close to the Gulf of Mexico.

Look at the **historical map** of New Orleans in 1798. A historical map shows a place at a particular time in history. At the top of the map, you can see Lake Pontchartrain. In the bottom right-hand corner, you see a part of the Mississippi River. On the north side of the river's curve is a fort originally built to protect the French settlers against threats from England and Spain.

1. Which part of New Orleans was more heavily settled in 1798, the north or the south?

2. What is the name of the swampy area between Lake Pontchartrain and the Mississippi River?

3. Swamps are found in low-lying areas. Which area of New Orleans has higher ground, the area near the river or the area near the lake?

By comparing a historical map with a modern map, you can see how a place has changed over time. Often, a modern map will still show some old landmarks. Most modern cities still have streets and other features that existed long ago. But the modern map will show many changes as well.

Look at the modern map of New Orleans to the right. It shows Lake Pontchartrain and the Mississippi River. Here, however, you can see more streets, many of them in areas that were swampland long ago. Over time, the city built **levees**—high barriers to hold back the floodwaters of the river and the lake. But when the water is higher or stronger than the levees can withstand, then these low, swampy areas are in danger of flooding. This is what happened in 2005 as a result of Hurricane Katrina.

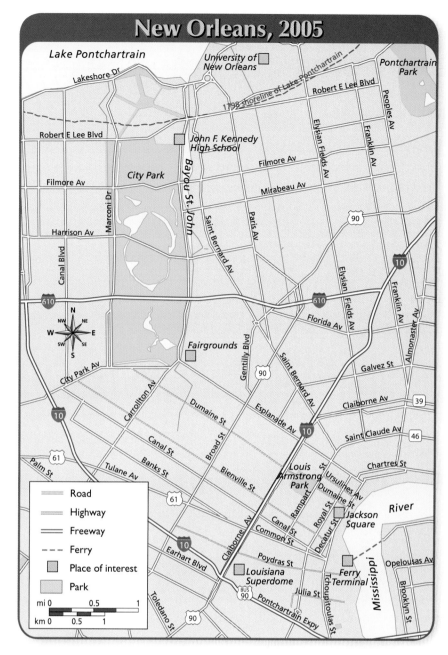

New Orleans along the Mississippi River

Use both maps of New Orleans to help answer these questions.

4. What is the old name of the land on which the University of New Orleans, John F. Kennedy High School, and City Park were all built?

5. What is the name of the square now located where the fort was in 1798?

6. Name two streets on the modern map in the location of the 1798 fort.

7. What bodies of water on the historic map are still on the 2005 map?

Population Change Over Time

In 1763, Spain gained control of the huge region called the Louisiana Territory. But Spain gave the territory back to France in 1801. The United States then bought it from France in 1803. The only major city in the territory at that time was New Orleans, but it gave the United States control of the Mississippi River. As the city became an important port for trade, many immigrants arrived from Europe. (An immigrant is a person who moves from one country to another to make a new home.) During the 1800s the city's population grew. By 1840, New Orleans was the fourth largest city in the United States. Immigrants continued to arrive into the early 1900s. As the city grew, its population density grew as well.

This chart shows population growth in New Orleans from 1820 through 2000. The numbers across the bottom of the chart identify years. The figures on the left show the number of people. As you can see, the population of New Orleans increased until 1960. It then dropped because many people began moving out of the city to the suburbs.

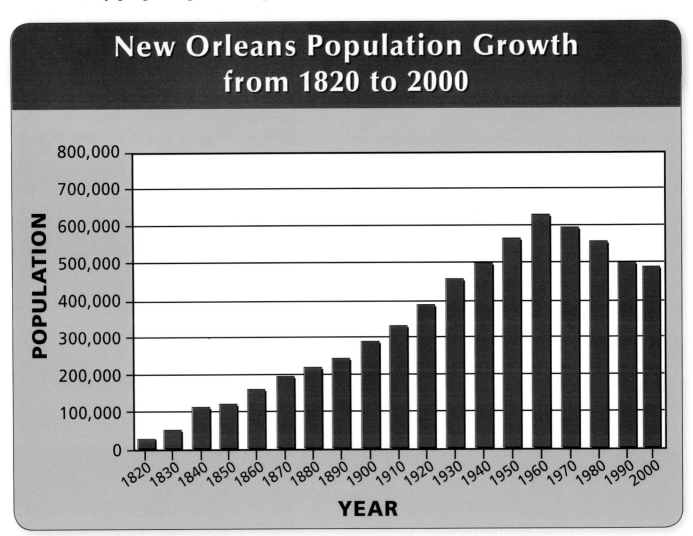

Look at the population graph above and answer the following questions.

8. In 1820 about 25,000 people lived in New Orleans. About how many lived there in 1850?

9. About how much did the population grow between 1910 and 1940?

10. About how many people did New Orleans lose between 1970 and 2000?

A Natural Disaster Strikes

Hurricane Katrina hit New Orleans and nearby areas on August 29, 2005. Heavy winds and rains did a lot of damage. For New Orleans, however, the biggest problem was the flooding that occurred after the storm. Levees protecting the city broke. The waters of Lake Pontchartrain poured into New Orleans, flooding 80% of the city. In some neighborhoods, water reached the tops of houses.

The shaded part of this map shows the areas that flooded.

11. Which neighborhood was underwater, Filmore or Marigny?

12. The French Quarter is the famous historic part of the city. Was this area flooded?

13. Were most houses built near the banks of the Mississippi River flooded?

14. Compare this map to the one on page 40. What do you notice about the areas that flooded compared to those that did not flood?

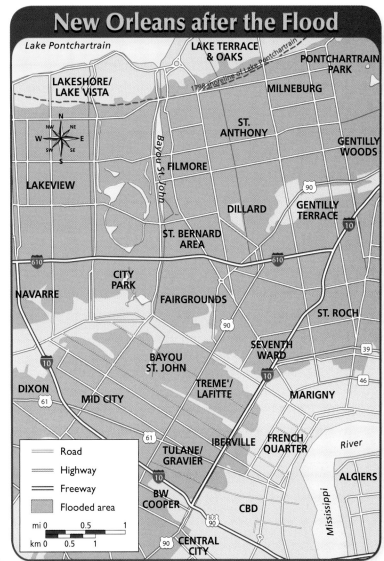

New Orleans after the Flood

Lake Pontchartrain · LAKE TERRACE & OAKS · PONTCHARTRAIN PARK · LAKESHORE/LAKE VISTA · 1798 shoreline of Lake Pontchartrain · MILNEBURG · ST. ANTHONY · GENTILLY WOODS · FILMORE · LAKEVIEW · DILLARD · GENTILLY TERRACE · ST. BERNARD AREA · Bayou St. John · CITY PARK · NAVARRE · FAIRGROUNDS · ST. ROCH · SEVENTH WARD · BAYOU ST. JOHN · DIXON · MID CITY · TREME'/LAFITTE · MARIGNY · IBERVILLE · FRENCH QUARTER · River · TULANE/GRAVIER · ALGIERS · BW COOPER · CBD · CENTRAL CITY · Mississippi

Legend:
— Road
— Highway
— Freeway
▨ Flooded area
mi 0   0.5   1
km 0   0.5   1

Skill Builder

Review

Use all three maps from this chapter to help answer these questions.

1. Would a classroom at John F. Kennedy High School, near City Park, have been underwater after Hurricane Katrina?

2. Was the area where the fort was in 1798 flooded in 2005?

3. Find the University of New Orleans. In 1798, was this area a fort or a swamp?

4. Find the ferry terminal on the Mississippi River. Was this area a swamp or a part of town in 1798?

Try It Yourself

Find three places in New Orleans that were flooded during Hurricane Katrina. Then find these areas on the 1798 map. Were these areas part of Cypress Swamp, part of the fort, or part of the town?

The United States is sometimes called a nation of **immigrants**. Many people living in the U.S. today moved here from other countries or have ancestors who came here from other parts of the world. Since colonial times, people from around the world have come to the United States seeking freedom, refuge, and a better life for themselves and their children.

People from many different **ethnic groups** have immigrated to the United States. An ethnic group is a group of people who share the same language and culture. Look at the map that shows the major ethnic groups in the thirteen colonies. The colors on the map show where each group had settled by 1755.

1. To which ethnic group did most people in the colonies belong in 1755?

2. What ethnic group settled mostly in New York City and along the Hudson River?

3. Name three ethnic groups that settled in North Carolina.

4. At the time shown on the map, almost all people of African descent were slaves brought to the colonies by force, not by choice. According to the map, which colonies relied most on slave labor?

5. As the colonists moved west, they moved away from the coast and toward the Appalachian Mountains. What ethnic group settled most in mountainous areas?

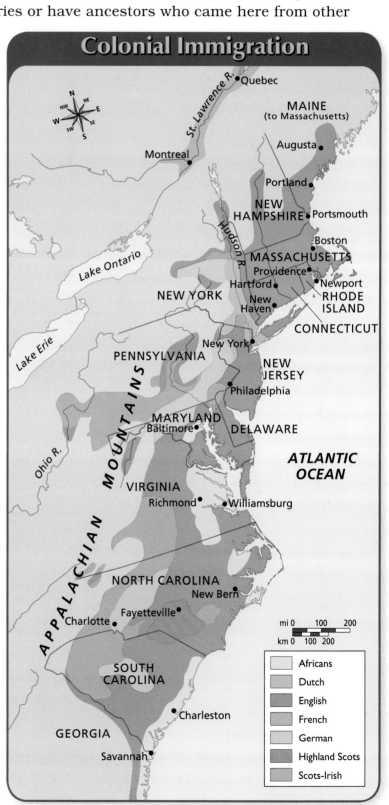

Colonial Immigration

Africans
Dutch
English
French
German
Highland Scots
Scots-Irish

The United States still has many immigrants from around the world. Many people who were born in the United States have immigrant parents, grandparents, or great-grandparents. One of the largest ethnic groups in the United States today is made up of **Latinos** (luh-TEE-nos), sometimes referred to as Hispanic people. Latinos come from Latin America, a term that generally includes the North and South American countries south of the United States, where languages based on Latin are spoken.

This map shows which states have the largest percentage of Latino people. Look at the colors on the map key. The darker shades are states that have higher percentages of Hispanics. The lighter shades are states that have lower percentages of Hispanics.

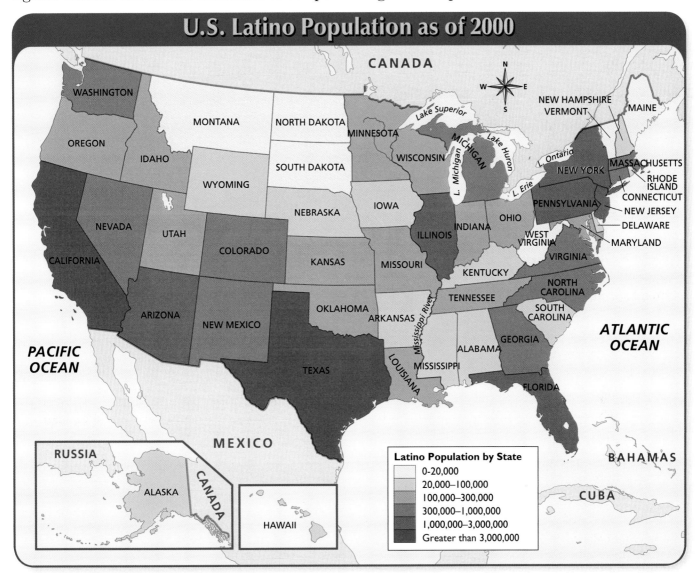

The map above shows the Latino population in each state as of the year 2000. Use the map key to help you answer the following questions.

6. Which state has a higher Latino population, Texas or Virginia?

7. Which state has a lower Latino population, Ohio or Illinois?

8. Which two states west of the Mississippi River have the largest Latino populations?

9. The biggest urban areas in the United States are located in New York, California, Illinois, Texas, Pennsylvania, and Florida. Do these states have high or low Latino populations?

The bar graphs below show the five countries from which the largest number of immigrants came to the United States in a particular decade. The bars and the numbers (on the left side of each graph) show how many people came from each country. You have to estimate the numbers. For example, between 1821 and 1830, about 25,000 immigrants came from the United Kingdom to the United States.

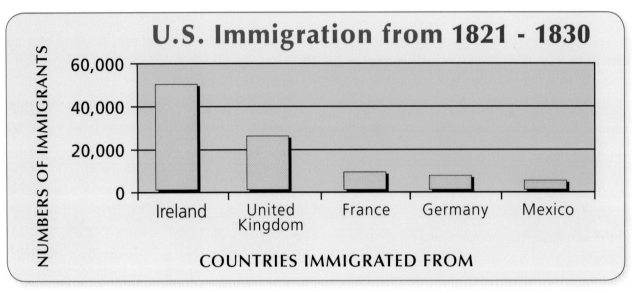

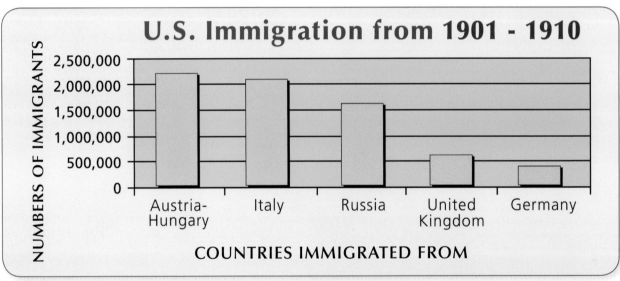

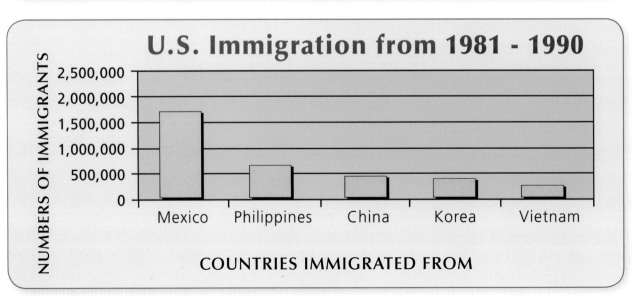

10. From what country did the most immigrants come between 1821 and 1830?

11. From what country did the most immigrants come between 1901 and 1910?

12. From what country did the most immigrants come between 1981 and 1990?

13. Between 1901 and 1910, did more immigrants come from Russia or the United Kingdom?

14. During which decade did the most immigrants come to the United States from the United Kingdom?

15. Between 1821 and 1830, about how many immigrants came from France, 21,000 or 8,500?

16. Did more Latino immigrants come to the United States between 1821-1830 or between 1981-1990?

The Statue of Liberty in New York Harbor welcomed many immigrants from Europe.

Skill Builder

Review

1. Name at least three ethnic groups in the thirteen colonies.

Use the charts on page 46 and the world map on pages 66-67 to help answer the following questions.

2. Between 1901 and 1910, did more immigrants come from Europe or Asia?

3. Between 1981 and 1990, leaving out Mexico, did more immigrants come from Europe or Asia?

Try It Yourself

Do immigrants make up part of your family? Where do your relatives and ancestors come from? Talk with family members to identify the immigrants in your past or present. Use the world map on pages 66-67 to locate where they came from.

Growing to Fifty States

Key Words: acquisition, treaty, annex, contiguous

In 1776, a group of British colonies in North America declared their independence. Those thirteen colonies became the first states of the United States of America. Today, there are fifty states covering more than five times the land area of the original colonies. This growth did not happen all at once. The map below shows how the United States grew. The colored areas show each **acquisition**—an addition of land to the country. It also shows when the land was acquired and the country that owned or controlled it before.

The first big acquisition was in 1803—in the Louisiana Purchase, the United States doubled in size when it bought a huge tract of land from France. Soon the U.S. acquired Florida in a **treaty** (*a formal agreement between two states or countries*) with Spain. In 1845, the United States annexed Texas. To **annex** means to add onto something—in this case, to add land to an existing country.

Growth of the United States

1. At the end of the American Revolution, Great Britain ceded (*which means "gave up, turned over"*) much land to the United States. What was the western boundary of the land that Great Britain ceded in 1783?

2. Name three territories that were gained by treaty.

3. What was the last addition of land to the United States? In what year did this occur?

4. How many present-day states include land that was part of the Louisiana Purchase?

By the mid-1850s, the United States had all the territory that we now call the **contiguous** 48 states. Contiguous means "touching" or "connected to." As you can see on the map on page 48, all the land of the United States, except for Alaska and Hawaii, was acquired by 1853. Each of the current 48 states in that land touches at least one other state. The United States acquired Alaska and Hawaii in the late 1800s.

The newly acquired lands did not become states right away. First, the lands were organized into territories. Once a territory had enough settlers, it could ask to become a state. When a territory became a state, its citizens could elect people to represent them in Congress. The map below shows when each of the fifty states officially joined the United States.

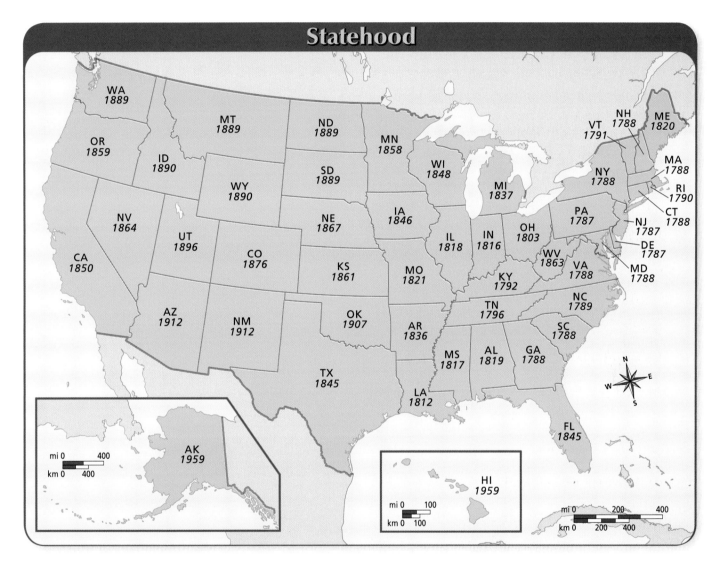

5. Name three states that became states after 1880.

6. Identify three states that became states between 1780 and 1800.

7. Look at the present-day states that were originally part of the Louisiana Purchase.

   Which became a state first? Which became a state last?

8. In what year did California become a state?

9. What two states were admitted to the Union most recently? How long have they been states?

Capital Cities

Every state has a capital city where elected officials meet to make state laws and run the state government. In some states, the capital city is also the largest city. For example, Boston is both the capital of Massachusetts and the largest city in the state. In most states, however, the capital city is not the biggest city. For example, Oregon's capital is Salem but Portland is the largest city in the state.

10. Study the map of states and their capitals, shown by stars. Try to make a mental map that stays in your head. Challenge yourself to fill in a blank map of the United States with the names of all 50 states and capitals.

The capitol building in Sacramento, California's state capital

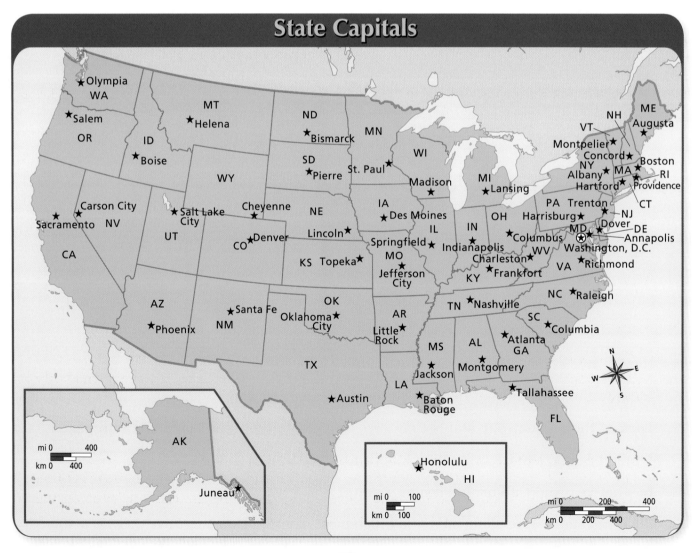

Can you figure out which states are described below? Use the maps in this chapter to help.

11. This state became a territory as part of the Louisiana Purchase in 1803 and a state in 1867. Its capital is Lincoln.

12. After being acquired in the Treaty of Paris, this territory became a state in 1792. Its capital is a very short drive south from the Ohio River.

13. This state was part of the Oregon Country. It became a state in 1889. Its capital is on an inlet from the ocean.

A photo of the great land rush in the Oklahoma Territory in 1893

14. This group of islands was the last land to be acquired by the United States. It was also the last to become a state in 1959.

15. This southeastern state became a state much later than other states around it. It was once claimed by Spain.

16. Mexico controlled this territory until 1848. It became a state in 1864.

17. A part of this state was ceded (*given to*) the United States by Great Britain in 1818. Its capital is Bismarck.

Skill Builder

Review

1. Was your state one of the original 13 colonies? What country or countries once claimed land in your state?

2. In what year was your state admitted to the Union?

3. What body of water is at the southernmost part of the lands gained in the Louisiana Purchase? In what year did the United States gain the rest of the land along this body of water? From which countries was the land acquired?

Try It Yourself

Did you know that the United States still has territories that are not states?
Go to *http://www.firstgov.gov/Agencies/State_and_Territories.shtml* to find out what these territories are, where they are located, and more. Then check the list of state links on the same page. One of the places listed is NOT a state! Which one is it?

Activity 13 — Our Nation's Capital

Key Words: National Mall, memorial

Soon after the American Revolution ended, lawmakers meeting in Philadelphia agreed that they needed to establish a capital city for the new nation. But where? They decided that the new national capital should be part of no state. They set aside land and called it the District of Columbia (honoring Columbus). George Washington, the newly elected president, thought it would be best to build the capital in the middle of the country, which at that time was on the east coast, near the Chesapeake Bay. Washington chose a site on the banks of the Potomac River.

1. About how many miles is it from Washington, D.C., to the northern border of Maine? How many miles is it from Washington, D.C., to the southern border of Georgia?

2. How far west had settlement extended by 1780?

3. What country held lands south of Georgia and west of the Mississippi River?

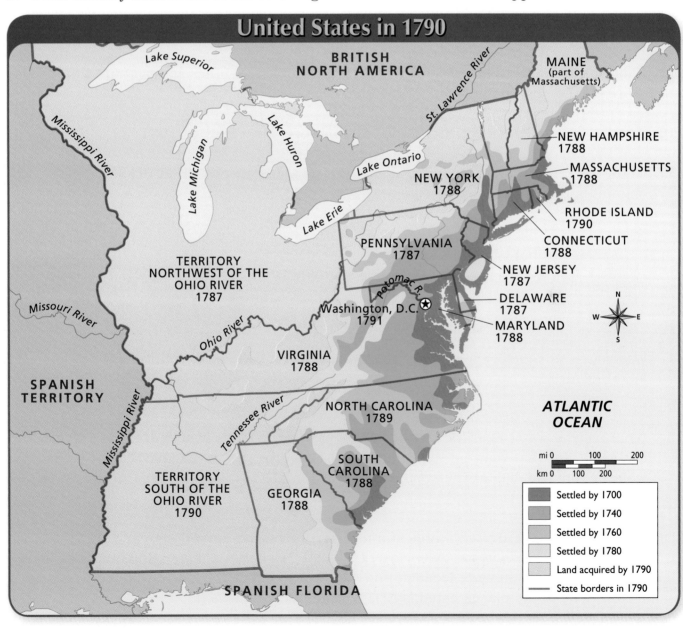

United States in 1790

Andrew Ellicott and Benjamin Banneker surveyed the site of the new capital. (To survey is to use special tools to measure the shape and area of land.) Pierre L'Enfant (lahn-FAHN), a French engineer and architect, planned the layout of much of the new city. He planned for the Capitol Building, the place where lawmakers meet, to be at the city's center. The map below shows L'Enfant's plan. He designed the **National Mall**, a long, grassy park to the west of the Capitol. The White House (then called the President's House) is to the north of the Mall. Wide avenues extend from the Capitol like the spokes of a bicycle wheel. L'Enfant also designed the circles that form the intersections where streets come together.

George Washington

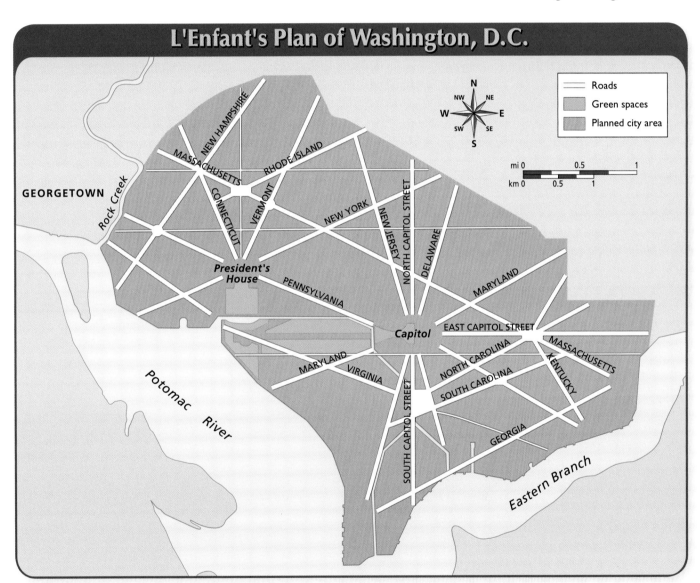

4. What building formed the center of L'Enfant's plans?

5. In what direction would you walk to go from the Capitol to the Potomac River?

6. What are all of the diagonal streets in the city named after?

7. What are the names of the streets that extend directly north, south, and east from the Capitol Building?

Today, the major government buildings in our nation's capital, Washington, D.C., are recognized by people around the world. The city also has many monuments and **memorials** that honor people and events from the country's history. Three of the best known include the Washington Monument, the Lincoln Memorial, and the Jefferson Memorial. Thousands of people from all over the country and the world visit Washington to see the buildings, monuments, memorials, and museums.

The Washington Monument

The Capitol Building

Washington, D.C., is not a state, and is not part of any state. The city was first planned as the place where the president, the Supreme Court, and Congress would meet, so no one thought that very many people would live there. Today, however, more than half a million people live in the city. But because Washington, D.C., is not a state, its people cannot send representatives to Congress.

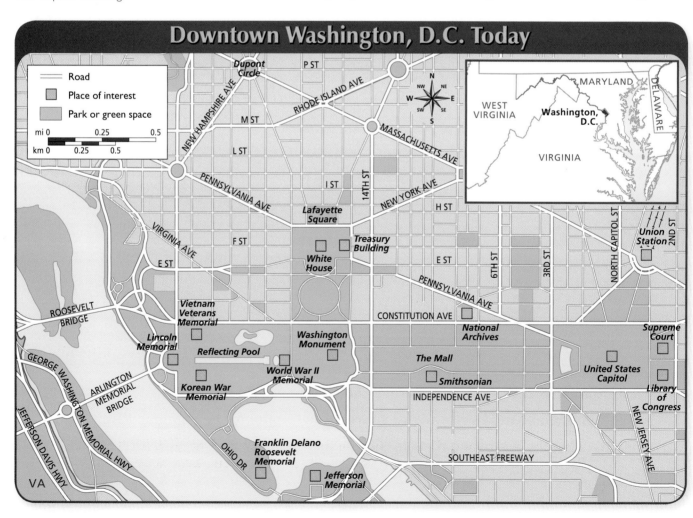

Downtown Washington, D.C. Today

54

Look at the map on the opposite page and answer the following questions.

8. What two states surround Washington, D.C.?

9. Name three monuments or memorials on this map.

10. If you wanted to walk directly from the U.S. Capitol to the White House, what street would you take?

11. About how far is it from the Washington Monument to the White House?

12. If you are standing in Lafayette Square and looking south, what building do you see?

13. If a senator leaves work at the Capitol for a meeting at the Treasury Building, about how far will he or she have to walk?

14. Name four avenues named after states.

15. Are any streets on this map named for western states? Why or why not? (Remember the original part of the city was planned in 1791.)

The Jefferson Memorial

Skill Builder

Review

1. Why isn't Washington, D.C., located within a state?

2. Name two monuments or memorials in Washington, D.C..

3. The people of Washington, D.C., do not have representatives in Congress. Why not?

4. What river runs to the west of the Lincoln Memorial?

Try It Yourself

Plan a trip to Washington, D.C. Start at the Capitol Building. Choose five other buildings you'd like to visit. Find them on the map, and write the directions and distances you will walk to visit each one.

Activity 14 Regions

Key Words: region, irrigation, climate region, economic region, political region, vegetation region, culture, cultural region

A national weather report is on the television. The forecaster is saying, "In the West, you can expect mild temperatures and lots of sunshine. Some storms will be moving into the Southeast. And in the Northeast, get out your umbrellas because rain is on the way."

West, Southeast, Northeast—those are names of some **regions** of the United States. Geographers organize the world by dividing it into regions. A region is an area with one or more features that it shares and that set it apart from the areas surrounding it.

For example, one simple way to organize the United States is into large regions based on location. Some maps group the states into four regions, some into five, or six, or even more. The map here identifies five main regions: the Northeast, the Southeast, the Midwest, the Southwest, and the West.

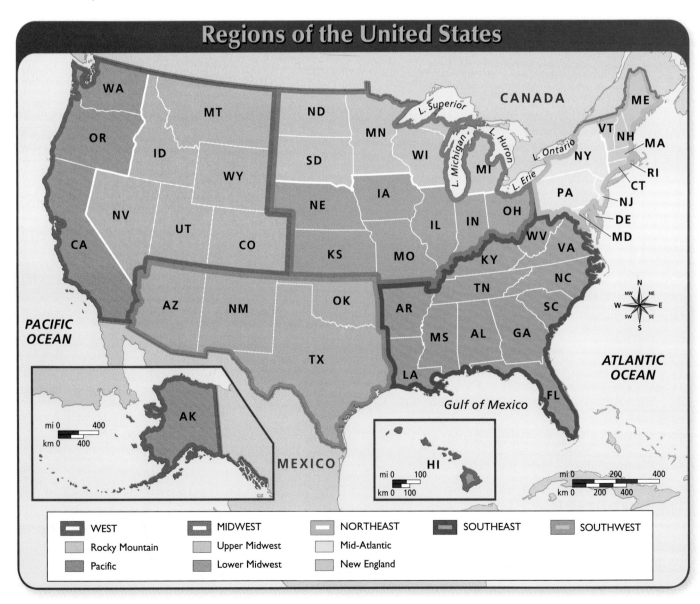

Regions of the United States

WEST	MIDWEST	NORTHEAST	SOUTHEAST	SOUTHWEST
Rocky Mountain	Upper Midwest	Mid-Atlantic		
Pacific	Lower Midwest	New England		

1. In which region is your state located?

2. Name two states in the Southwest.

3. Name two states in the West.

4. Ohio, Pennsylvania, and West Virginia touch each other, but they are in different regions. What region is each state in?

5. Which three regions touch Canada?

6. Identify two regions that touch Mexico.

7. In what region are Alaska and Hawaii located?

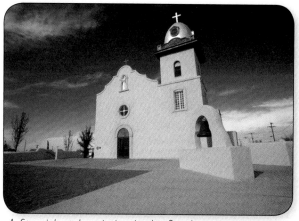

A Spanish-style mission in the Southwest region

Let's look at one region to see how it shares certain features. Find the Southwest on the map on page 56. The Southwest is a land of cliffs, canyons, and mountains. Much of this region has a desert climate, with less than ten inches of rain per year. In the driest places, you won't see big green forests but instead cactus, shrubs, and a few small trees. Early Native Americans became experts at **irrigation** (bringing water to dry areas to help grow crops). Later, Spanish settlers from Mexico established towns around Catholic missions, and built ranches similar to their homes back in Mexico and Spain. Today you can see both Native American and Spanish influence in the art and architecture of the Southwest.

The desert in Arizona, in the Southwest region

Sometimes these big regions are divided into smaller regions. For example, as the map on page 56 shows, the vast West can be divided into the Pacific and Rocky Mountain regions. The Northeast can be divided into New England and the Mid-Atlantic.

A forest in the New England region

In contrast to the Southwest, in New England you'll find many dense forests. Native Americans—and, later, English settlers—cleared patches of these forests to farm. They built their homes from the abundant timber or from the stones they cleared from the rocky soil. As more settlers arrived, they made use of the natural harbors on the rugged coastline to become shipbuilders and traders. Factories grew in towns along rapid rivers. New England remains a region with both rural areas of forests and mountains, and urban areas of manufacturing and business.

There are many kinds and sizes of regions. For example, we can organize the United States into the following kinds of regions:

- **climate regions:** based on the average temperature and rainfall in different areas (See page 13 for a map of climate regions of the U.S., also called climate zones.)
- **economic regions:** based on the kinds of work people do in different places—for example, an agricultural region with many farmers, or a manufacturing region where many people work in factories
- **political regions:** areas with clear boundaries in which the people share a government; within the United States, each of the fifty states is a political region
- **vegetation regions:** areas where similar kinds of plants grow, such as grasses or evergreen forests

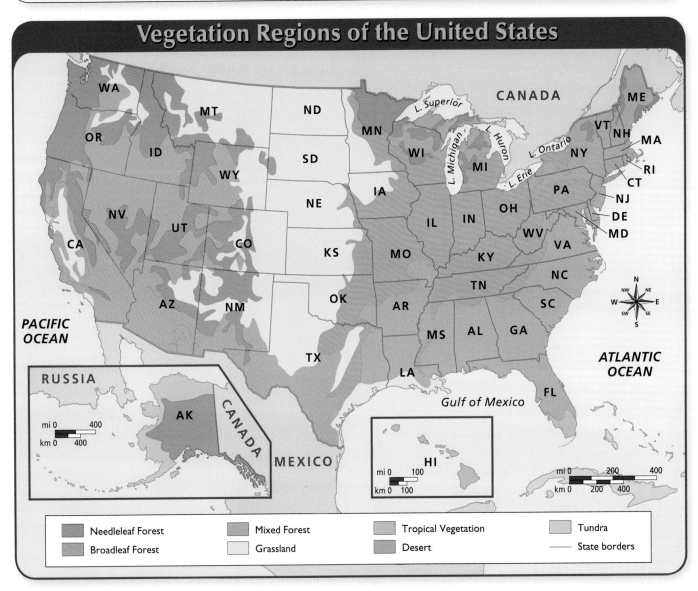

Vegetation Regions of the United States

Use the map above to answer the following questions.

8. What are the only two states with tropical vegetation?

9. California has four different vegetation regions. Name another state with four different vegetation regions.

10. A tundra is a treeless plain in a very cold area. What is the only state with a tundra vegetation region?

Regions can also be based on **culture**. Culture is a people's way of life. It includes their language, customs, art, foods, clothing, religion, and more. A **cultural region** is an area where most people share a common way of life.

This map shows Native American cultural regions. Each cultural region had features that made it different from the other regions. For example, historically, all Native Americans used the resources around them to live, but many groups in the Northeast lived in log houses, while many people of the Great Plains used buffalo hides to make tepees.

11. Name three Native American groups in the Southeastern cultural region.

12. What are two Native American groups in what is now Utah?

Native American Cultural Regions

Legend:
- Northwest Coast
- Plateau
- California
- Northeast
- Great Basin
- Great Plains
- Southeast
- Southwest
- Present-day state borders

Skill Builder

Review

1. Look at the map of U.S. regions on page 56. If you travel directly from New Mexico to New York, what regions will you go through?

2. New England is part of a bigger region. What is this bigger region often called?

3. What kind of region is based upon common language, customs, clothing, art, and religion—a political region or a cultural region?

4. What kind of region is based on the kinds of work people do—a cultural or economic region?

Try It Yourself

Look at the map of U.S. regions on page 56. Which region do you live in? What features characterize your region? Make a poster about your region. Include a map and pictures to represent the shared features of your region.

Map Review

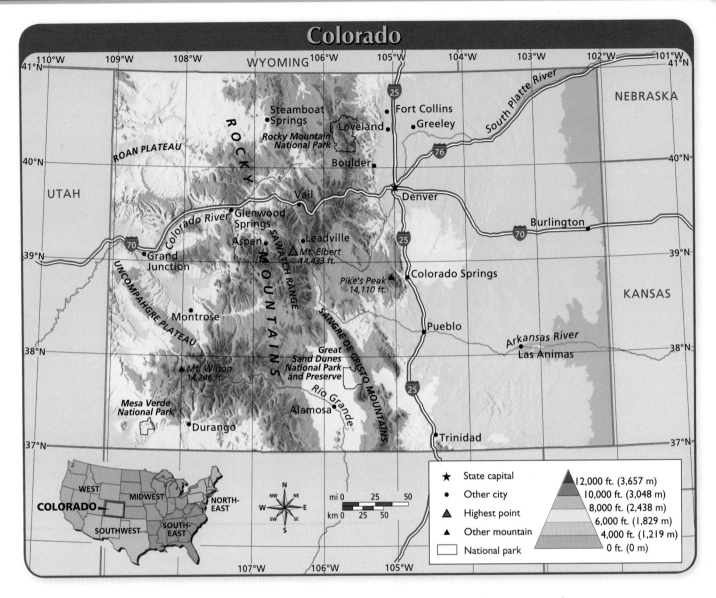

Colorado

Use the map of Colorado above to answer the following questions.

1. In which region of the United States is the state of Colorado located, the Midwest or the West?
2. Which river starts in the Rocky Mountains and flows west?
3. What is the highest point in Colorado?
4. What interstate highway would you use to drive west from Burlington to Grand Junction?
5. Some of the longest rivers in the United States begin in the Rocky Mountains. What is the beginning of a river called?
6. What national park is located in the southwest corner of the state?
7. Name two landforms in the state of Colorado.
8. About how many miles is it from the capital city of Denver to Trinidad?
9. Which city is at a higher elevation, Pueblo or Durango?
10. Which city is closer to 40° N, 105° W, Colorado Springs or Boulder?
11. Name a city at about the same latitude as Loveland.
12. Name a city at the same longitude as Montrose.

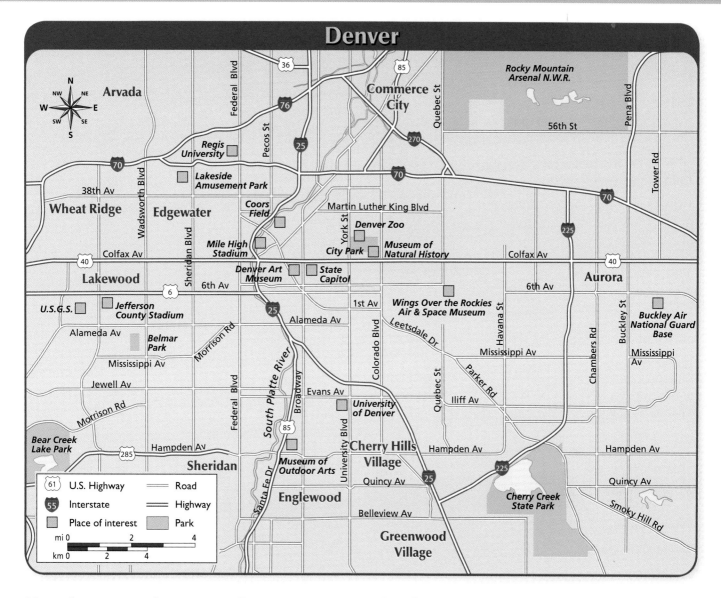

Denver

Use the map of Denver above to answer the following questions.

13. Is the state Capitol east or west of the South Platte River?

14. Does this map of Denver have a larger or smaller scale than a map of the U.S.?

15. In what direction would you travel on Route 70 to go from Wadsworth Blvd. to Tower Road?

16. Name two colleges or universities located in Denver.

17. Which park is further north, Belmar Park or City Park?

18. How far in miles is it from the University of Denver to Jefferson County Stadium? Measure first in a straight line (as the crow flies). Then measure using roads. Which way is longer? By how much?

19. What direction is Cherry Creek State Park from Denver?

20. Name two museums south of State Route 40 and east of Interstate 25.

21. Name the streets you would travel on to go from the Museum of Outdoor Arts to the state Capitol.

22. Name two of the sports arenas or stadiums located in Denver.

Glossary

absolute location: the exact location of a place on Earth, often identified by the latitude and longitude of the place

acquisition: an addition of land to a country

agriculture: the practice of growing crops and raising animals such as cattle or sheep

animal resources: fish, cattle, pigs, and other animals we use for food, clothing, etc.

annex: to add on to something

basin: all the land drained by a river and by all the streams flowing into the river

bay: a small body of water partly surrounded by land, usually smaller than a gulf

canals: manmade waterways used for transportation

cardinal directions: the four main directions (north, south, east, and west)

climate: the usual pattern of weather in a place over a very long period of time

climate region: an area with similar average temperatures and rainfall

climograph: a graph that shows the average temperature and precipitation in a certain place during a year

coastal plain: low, flat land near the ocean

compass rose: a symbol showing the directions on a map

contiguous: touching or connected to

coordinates: points on a map where lines of latitude and longitude intersect

coordinate system: lines of latitude and longitude that come together to form a grid system

culture: a people's way of life that includes language, customs, art, foods, clothing, religion, and more

cultural region: an area where people share a common way of life

delta: the soft, silty land where a river widens out before emptying into another river, a lake, or the ocean

desert: a dry, often sandy area that gets very little rain

distortion: the stretching or bending of an image away from its true shape

economic region: an area in which many people do similar kinds of work, such as farming or manufacturing

elevation: the height of the land above sea level, also called *altitude*

Equator: an imaginary line around the middle of the Earth, halfway between the North and the South Poles

estuary: a partly enclosed body of water where fresh river water mixes with salt water from the ocean, bay, or gulf

ethnic group: a group of people that share a common language and culture

export: to send goods to another place

fossil fuel: fuels such as oil and natural gas

gulf: a part of a sea or ocean that extends into the land, usually larger than a bay

harbor: a sheltered area along a coast

hemisphere: one half of the Earth; the Earth can be divided into four hemispheres (Eastern, Western, Northern, and Southern)

hill: a raised area on Earth, not as high as a mountain

historical maps: maps that show what a place was like in an earlier time

immigrant: a person who moves permanently from one country to another

import: to bring goods in from another place

intermediate directions: the directions in between the cardinal directions (northwest, northeast, southwest, and southeast)

irrigation: the practice of bringing water to dry areas to help grow crops

island: land that is completely surrounded by water

lake: a body of water, usually fresh water, surrounded by land on all sides

landform: a physical feature on the Earth, such as a mountain, hill, or plateau

large scale: the view on a map that shows small, detailed areas of the Earth

latitude: lines that run east and west on a map or globe and measure distance north and south of the Equator; also called *parallels*

levee: a high barrier made to hold back flood waters of lakes or rivers

longitude: lines that run from the North Pole to the South Pole on a map or globe and measure distance east and west; also called *meridians*

map key: a guide to what the symbols on a map mean; also called a *legend*

map scale: the symbol on a map that shows how real distance on Earth compares to the distance on the map

megalopolis: a densely populated region made up of several cities and the surrounding areas

memorial: a place that honors people or historical events

migration: the movement of large groups of people from one place to another

mineral resources: materials such as copper or aluminum, often mined from the ground

mountain: the highest type of landform, higher than hills

mountain range: large groups of mountains

mouth: the end of a river, where it flows into a larger body of water

National Mall: the long grassy park directly west of the U.S. Capitol Building in Washington, D.C.

natural resources: materials we use that come from nature

nonrenewable resources: resources such as minerals and fossil fuels that cannot be replaced once they have been used

ocean: one of four large bodies of salt water on Earth

peak: a high mountain or the pointed top of one

peninsula: a body of land that is almost completely surrounded by water

piedmont: an area of land at the bottom of a mountain range

plain: a large area of mostly flat land with few trees

plant resources: plants we use, such as trees for lumber or crops for food

plateau: a large area of high, flat land

political region: an area with clear boundaries in which people share a government

population: the total number of people living in an area

population density: the number of people living in an area of a certain size

precipitation: moisture that falls to the Earth in various forms, such as rain, snow, sleet, and hail

prime meridian: an imaginary line that runs between the North and South Poles and divides the Earth into the Eastern and Western Hemispheres

projection: the way of showing the round Earth on a flat map

raw materials: resources used to make other products

region: an area with at least one feature that sets it apart from the areas surrounding it

relief map: a map that shows the higher and lower parts of an area

renewable resources: resources such as plants and animals that we can grow or raise more of as we use them

river: a large stream of fresh water that flows over land

rural: of or related to the countryside, farms, or farm life

small scale: the view on a map that shows large, less detailed areas of the Earth

source: the beginning of a river

suburbs: mostly residential communities just outside of cities

trade: the business of buying, selling, or exchanging goods

transportation map: a map that shows routes of travel and sometimes the means of getting from one place to another

triangular trade: the system of trading slaves and goods between Europe, Africa, and Europe's colonies in the Caribbean and in North and South America

urban: of or related to cities and city life

treaty: a formal agreement between two states or countries

tributary: a river that flows into another river

valley: a low area between mountains or hills

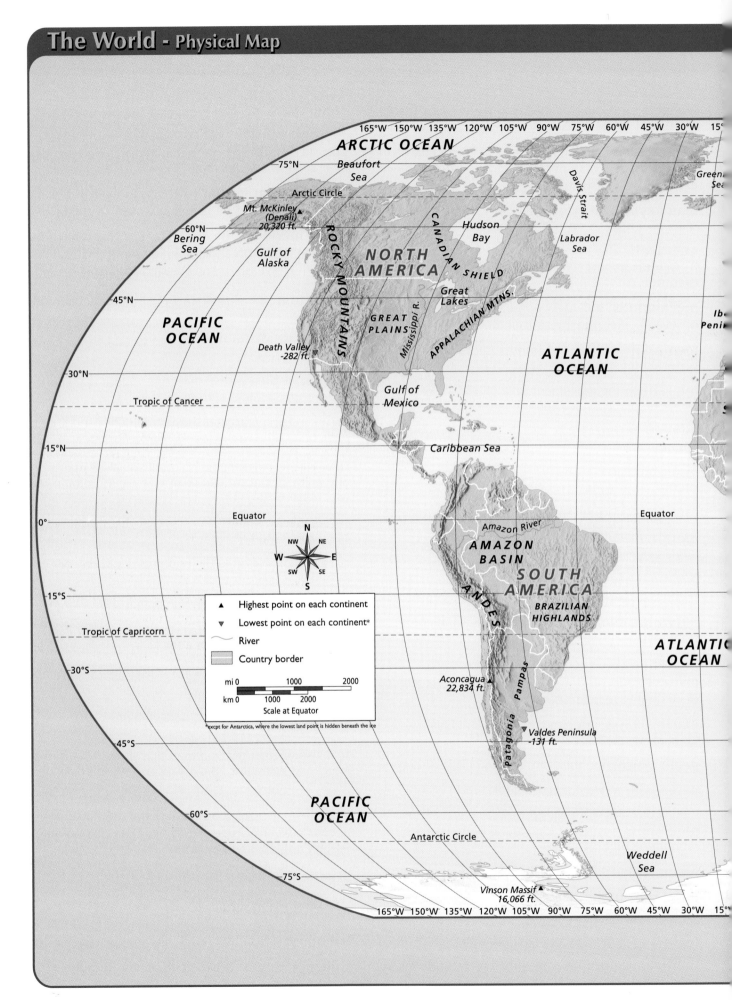

ARCTIC OCEAN

75°N · Beaufort Sea

Arctic Circle

Greenland Sea

Davis Strait

Mt. McKinley (Denali) 20,320 ft.

60°N · Bering Sea

Gulf of Alaska

ROCKY MOUNTAINS

NORTH AMERICA

CANADIAN SHIELD

Hudson Bay

Labrador Sea

45°N

PACIFIC OCEAN

GREAT PLAINS

Great Lakes

Mississippi R.

APPALACHIAN MTNS.

ATLANTIC OCEAN

Iberian Peninsula

Death Valley -282 ft.

30°N

Tropic of Cancer

Gulf of Mexico

15°N

Caribbean Sea

Equator

Amazon River

Equator

N
NW · NE
W · E
SW · SE
S

AMAZON BASIN

SOUTH AMERICA

ANDES

BRAZILIAN HIGHLANDS

15°S

▲ Highest point on each continent

▼ Lowest point on each continent*

〜 River

Country border

mi 0 · 1000 · 2000
km 0 · 1000 · 2000
Scale at Equator

*excpt for Antarctica, where the lowest land point is hidden beneath the ice

Tropic of Capricorn

ATLANTIC OCEAN

30°S

Aconcagua 22,834 ft.

Pampas

45°S

Patagonia

▼ Valdes Peninsula -131 ft.

PACIFIC OCEAN

60°S

Antarctic Circle

Weddell Sea

75°S

Vinson Massif ▲ 16,066 ft.

165°W 150°W 135°W 120°W 105°W 90°W 75°W 60°W 45°W 30°W 15°W

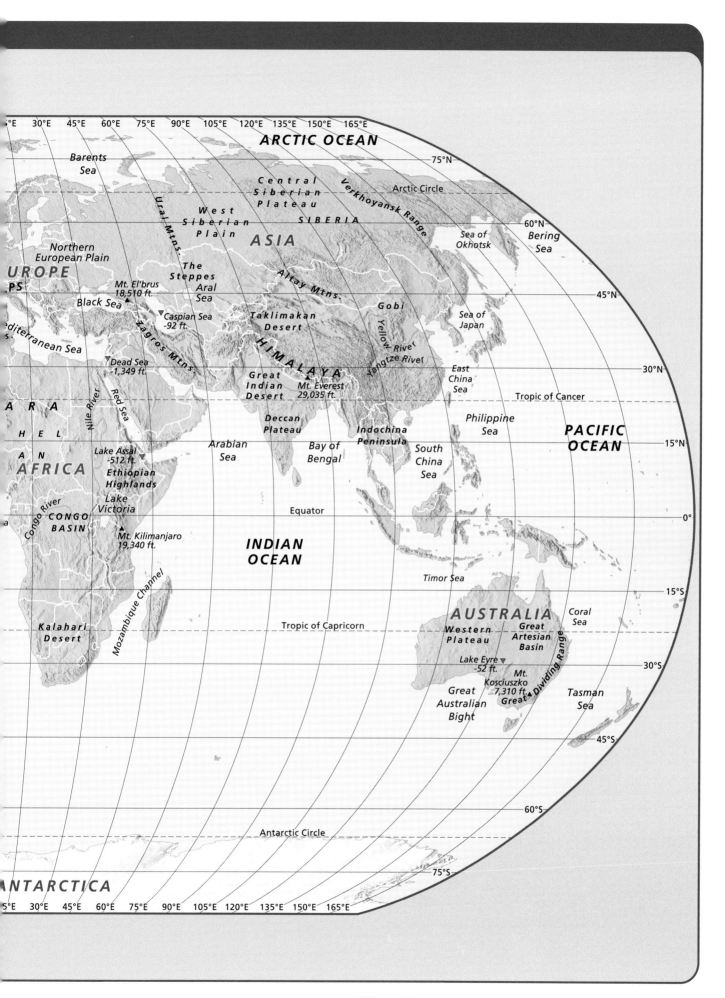

ARCTIC OCEAN

75°N

°E 30°E 45°E 60°E 75°E 90°E 105°E 120°E 135°E 150°E 165°E

Barents
Sea

Central
Siberian
Plateau

Verkhoyansk Range

Arctic Circle

60°N

West
Siberian
Plain

Ural Mtns.

SIBERIA

Sea of
Okhotsk

Bering
Sea

Northern
European Plain

ASIA

EUROPE

The
Steppes

Altay Mtns.

45°N

PS

Mt. El'brus
18,510 ft.

Aral
Sea

Gobi

Sea of
Japan

Black Sea

Caspian Sea
-92 ft.

Taklimakan
Desert

Yellow River

Mediterranean Sea

Zagros Mtns.

HIMALAYA

Yangtze River

East
China
Sea

30°N

Dead Sea
-1,349 ft.

Great
Indian
Desert

Mt. Everest
29,035 ft.

Tropic of Cancer

ARA

Nile River

Red Sea

Deccan
Plateau

Philippine
Sea

PACIFIC
OCEAN

HEL

Arabian
Sea

Bay of
Bengal

Indochina
Peninsula

15°N

AN

Lake Assal
-512 ft.

South
China
Sea

AFRICA

Ethiopian
Highlands

Lake
Victoria

Congo River

CONGO
BASIN

Equator

0°

Mt. Kilimanjaro
19,340 ft.

INDIAN
OCEAN

Timor Sea

15°S

Mozambique Channel

AUSTRALIA

Coral
Sea

Kalahari
Desert

Tropic of Capricorn

Western
Plateau

Great
Artesian
Basin

Great Dividing Range

Lake Eyre
-52 ft.

30°S

Great
Australian
Bight

Mt.
Kosciuszko
7,310 ft.
Great

Tasman
Sea

45°S

60°S

Antarctic Circle

75°S

ANTARCTICA

°E 30°E 45°E 60°E 75°E 90°E 105°E 120°E 135°E 150°E 165°E

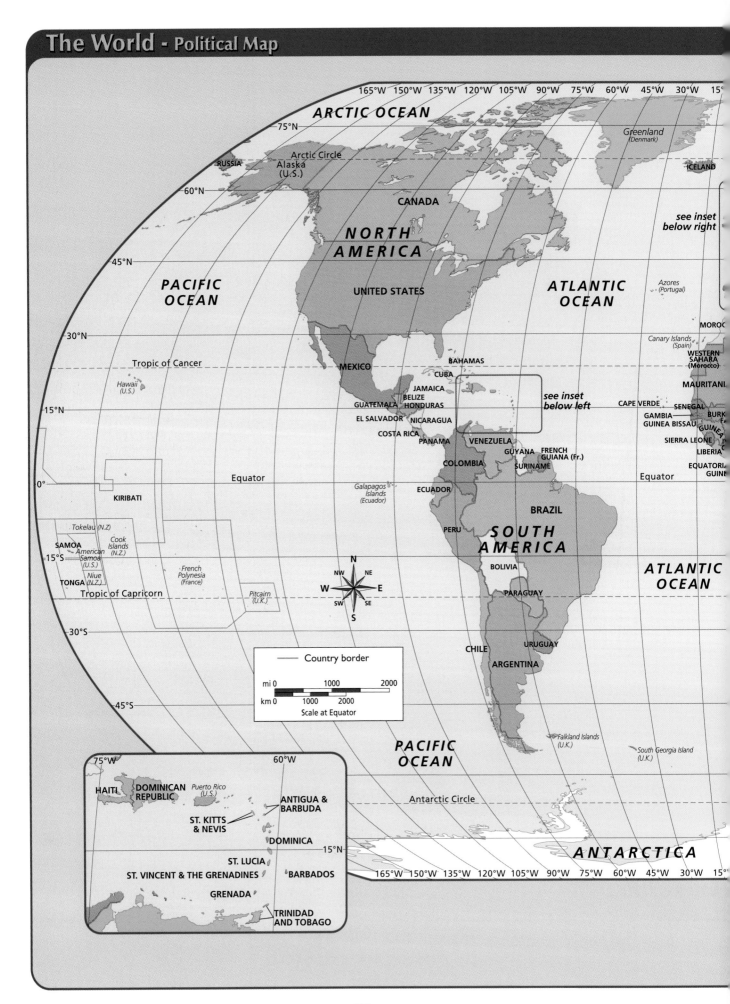

ARCTIC OCEAN

75°N

Greenland
(Denmark)

Arctic Circle
Alaska
(U.S.)

RUSSIA

ICELAND

60°N

CANADA

see inset
below right

NORTH
AMERICA

45°N

PACIFIC
OCEAN

ATLANTIC
OCEAN

Azores
(Portugal)

UNITED STATES

MOROC

30°N

Canary Islands
(Spain)

Tropic of Cancer

MEXICO

BAHAMAS

WESTERN
SAHARA
(Morocco)

Hawaii
(U.S.)

CUBA

MAURITANI

15°N

JAMAICA
BELIZE
HONDURAS

GUATEMALA

see inset
below left

CAPE VERDE

SENEGAL

GAMBIA
GUINEA BISSAU

BURK
F

EL SALVADOR

NICARAGUA

COSTA RICA

SIERRA LEONE

GUINEA

PANAMA

VENEZUELA

LIBERIA

GUYANA
FRENCH
GUIANA (Fr.)

EQUATORI
GUINE

COLOMBIA

SURINAME

Equator

KIRIBATI

Equator

Galapagos
Islands
(Ecuador)

ECUADOR

0°

BRAZIL

Tokelau (N.Z)

PERU

SOUTH
AMERICA

SAMOA

Cook
Islands
(N.Z.)

American
Samoa
(U.S.)

BOLIVIA

ATLANTIC
OCEAN

15°S

Niue
(N.Z.)

TONGA (N.Z.)

French
Polynesia
(France)

N

NW   NE

Tropic of Capricorn

Pitcairn
(U.K.)

W   E

PARAGUAY

SW   SE

S

30°S

Country border

CHILE

URUGUAY

mi 0   1000   2000

ARGENTINA

km 0   1000   2000

Scale at Equator

45°S

Falkland Islands
(U.K.)

South Georgia Island
(U.K.)

PACIFIC
OCEAN

75°W

60°W

HAITI

DOMINICAN
REPUBLIC

Puerto Rico
(U.S.)

ANTIGUA &
BARBUDA

Antarctic Circle

ANTARCTICA

ST. KITTS
& NEVIS

165°W 150°W 135°W 120°W 105°W 90°W 75°W 60°W 45°W 30°W 15°

DOMINICA

15°N

ST. LUCIA

ST. VINCENT & THE GRENADINES

BARBADOS

GRENADA

TRINIDAD
AND TOBAGO

165°W   150°W   135°W   120°W   105°W   90°W   75°W   60°W   45°W   30°W   15°

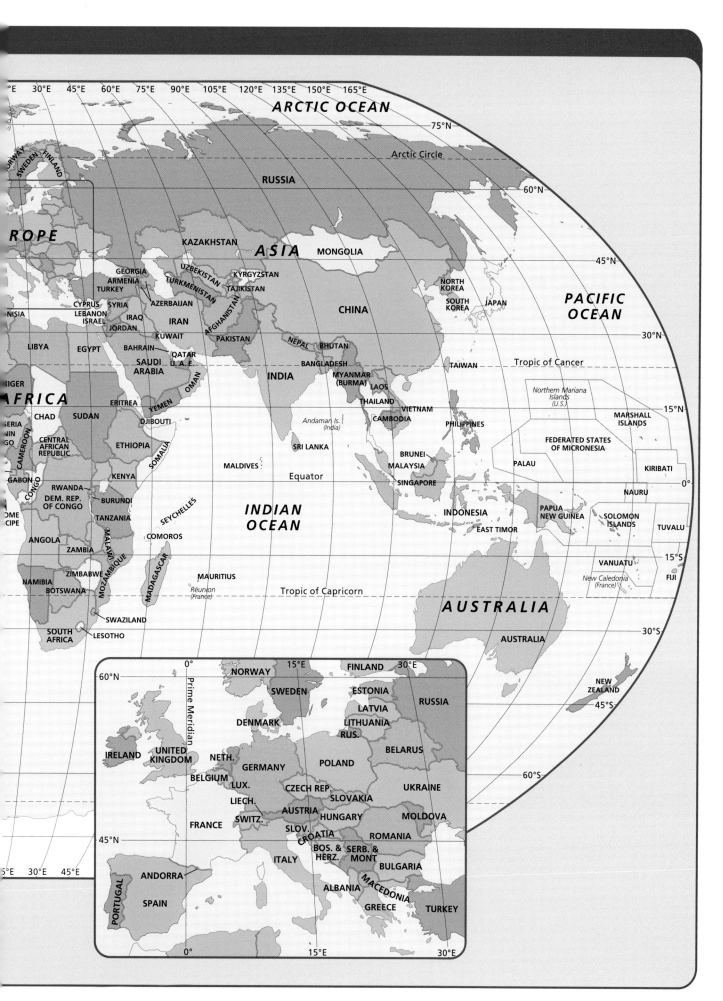

ARCTIC OCEAN

75°N

Arctic Circle

RUSSIA

60°N

EUROPE

KAZAKHSTAN ASIA MONGOLIA 45°N

GEORGIA
ARMENIA
TURKEY
UZBEKISTAN
KYRGYZSTAN
TURKMENISTAN
TAJIKISTAN
NORTH
KOREA
SOUTH
KOREA
JAPAN
PACIFIC
OCEAN

CYPRUS
LEBANON
ISRAEL
SYRIA
IRAQ
JORDAN
AZERBAIJAN
AFGHANISTAN
IRAN
CHINA
30°N

KUWAIT
BAHRAIN
QATAR
U.A.E.
PAKISTAN
NEPAL
BHUTAN
TAIWAN
Tropic of Cancer

LIBYA
EGYPT
SAUDI
ARABIA
OMAN
BANGLADESH
MYANMAR
(BURMA)
LAOS

AFRICA

NIGER
INDIA
THAILAND
VIETNAM
15°N

CHAD
SUDAN
ERITREA
YEMEN
DJIBOUTI
Andaman Is.
(India)
CAMBODIA
PHILIPPINES
Northern Mariana
Islands
(U.S.)
MARSHALL
ISLANDS

CENTRAL
AFRICAN
REPUBLIC
ETHIOPIA
SOMALIA
SRI LANKA
FEDERATED STATES
OF MICRONESIA

CAMEROON
GABON
CONGO
KENYA
MALDIVES
Equator
BRUNEI
MALAYSIA
SINGAPORE
PALAU
KIRIBATI
0°

SOME
CIPE
RWANDA
DEM. REP.
OF CONGO
BURUNDI
TANZANIA
SEYCHELLES
INDIAN
OCEAN
INDONESIA
PAPUA
NEW GUINEA
EAST TIMOR
SOLOMON
ISLANDS
NAURU
TUVALU

ANGOLA
ZAMBIA
MALAWI
COMOROS
MADAGASCAR
15°S
VANUATU
New Caledonia
(France)
FIJI

NAMIBIA
ZIMBABWE
BOTSWANA
MOZAMBIQUE
MAURITIUS
Réunion
(France)
Tropic of Capricorn
AUSTRALIA

SWAZILAND
SOUTH
AFRICA
LESOTHO
AUSTRALIA
30°S

NEW
ZEALAND
45°S

60°N
NORWAY
15°E
FINLAND
30°E
RUSSIA
SWEDEN
ESTONIA
LATVIA
LITHUANIA
RUS.
60°S

DENMARK
BELARUS

IRELAND
UNITED
KINGDOM
NETH.
GERMANY
POLAND

BELGIUM
LUX.
CZECH REP.
SLOVAKIA
UKRAINE

LIECH.
AUSTRIA
HUNGARY
MOLDOVA

FRANCE
SWITZ.
SLOV.
CROATIA
ROMANIA
45°N
BOS. &
HERZ.
SERB. &
MONT

ANDORRA
ITALY
BULGARIA

PORTUGAL
SPAIN
ALBANIA
MACEDONIA
GREECE
TURKEY

Prime Meridian

0°
15°E
30°E

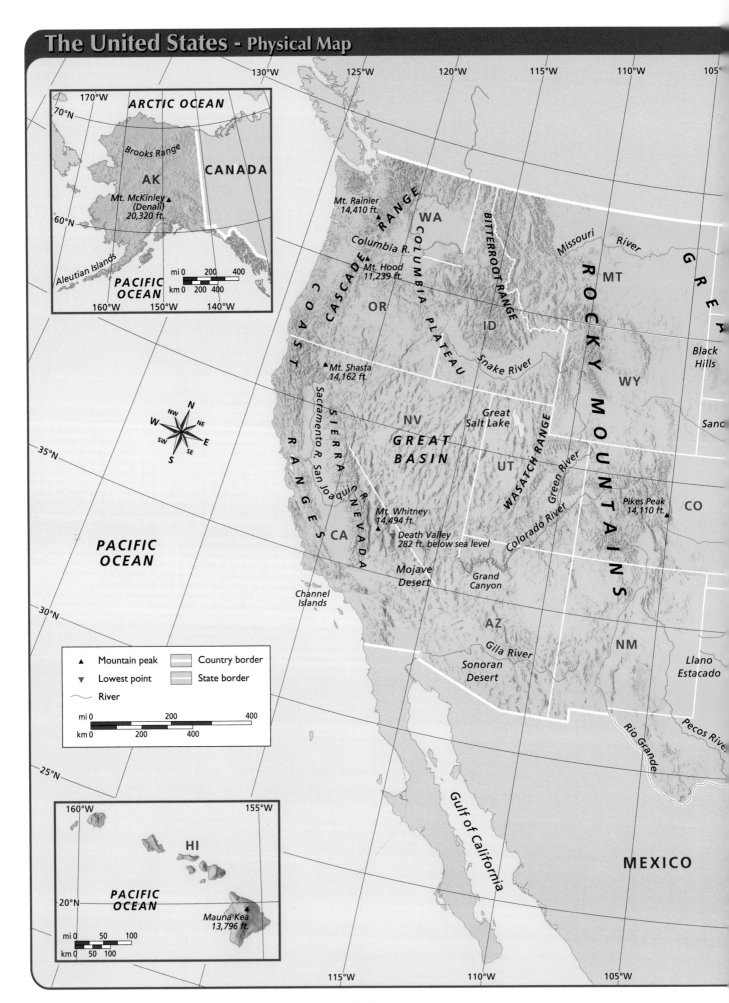

ARCTIC OCEAN

170°W
70°N

Brooks Range

AK   CANADA

Mt. McKinley
(Denali)
20,320 ft.

60°N

Aleutian Islands

PACIFIC
OCEAN

160°W   150°W   140°W

mi 0   200   400
km 0   200   400

130°W   125°W   120°W   115°W   110°W   105°W

Mt. Rainier
14,410 ft.   WA

RANGE

COLUMBIA

Columbia R.
Mt. Hood
11,239 ft.

BITTERROOT RANGE

Missouri   River

CASCADE

COAST

OR   COLUMBIA PLATEAU

ID   Snake River

G R E A

MT

ROCKY MOUNTAINS

Black
Hills

WY

Mt. Shasta
14,162 ft.

Sacramento R. San Joa

SIERRA

quin R.

NEVADA

NV   Great
Salt Lake

WASATCH RANGE

Green River

GREAT
BASIN   UT

Sanc

35°N

RANGES

Mt. Whitney
14,494 ft.   Death Valley
282 ft. below sea level

CA

Colorado River

Pikes Peak
14,110 ft.   CO

PACIFIC
OCEAN

Mojave
Desert

Grand
Canyon

N
NW   NE
W   E
SW   SE
S

Channel
Islands

30°N

AZ   NM

Gila River   Llano
Estacado

Sonoran
Desert

Mountain peak   Country border
Lowest point   State border
River

mi 0   200   400
km 0   200   400

Rio Grande   Pecos River

25°N

160°W   155°W

HI

20°N   PACIFIC
OCEAN

Mauna Kea
13,796 ft.

mi 0   50   100
km 0   50   100

Gulf of California

MEXICO

115°W   110°W   105°W

68

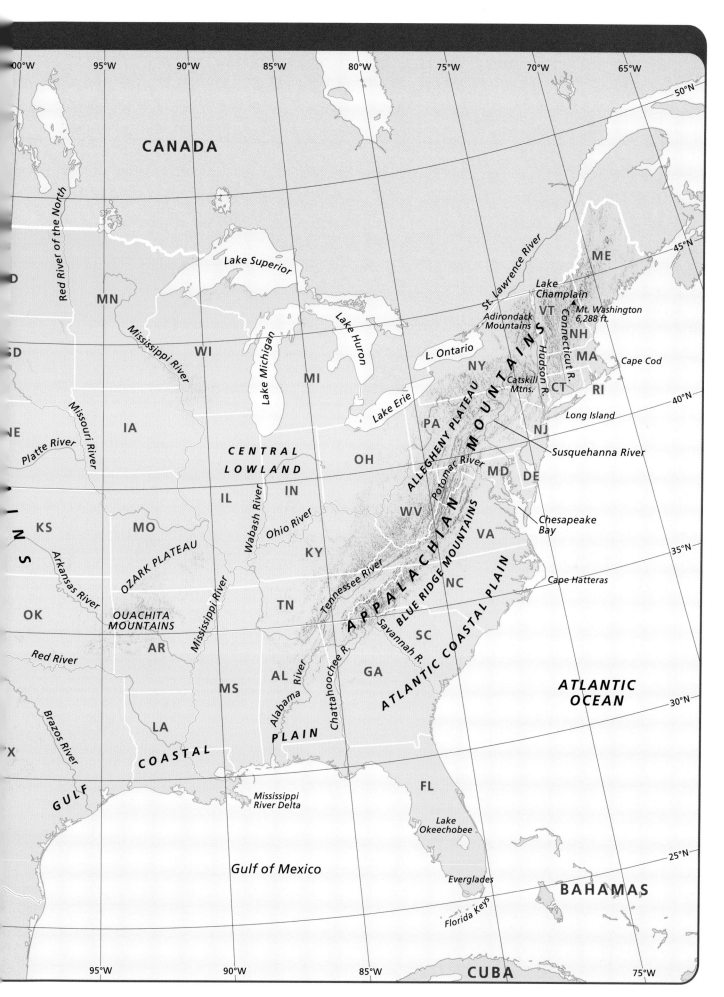

100°W 95°W 90°W 85°W 80°W 75°W 70°W 65°W

50°N
45°N
40°N
35°N
30°N
25°N

CANADA

Red River of the North

MN

Lake Superior

St. Lawrence River

ME

Lake Champlain

Mt. Washington
6,288 ft.

Adirondack
Mountains

VT
NH

Connecticut R.

Hudson R.

MA

Cape Cod

WI

Mississippi River

Lake Michigan

Lake Huron

L. Ontario

NY

Catskill
Mtns.

CT

RI

Lake Erie

PA

ALLEGHENY PLATEAU

Long Island

Missouri River

IA

CENTRAL
LOWLAND

OH

NJ

Susquehanna River

Platte River

Potomac River

MD

DE

Chesapeake
Bay

KS

MO

IL

Wabash River

IN

Ohio River

WV

VA

OZARK PLATEAU

KY

Tennessee River

BLUE RIDGE MOUNTAINS

NC

Cape Hatteras

Arkansas River

Mississippi River

TN

APPALACHIAN

MOUNTAINS

OK

OUACHITA
MOUNTAINS

AR

SC

ATLANTIC COASTAL PLAIN

Red River

AL

Alabama River

Chattahoochee R.

Savannah R.

GA

ATLANTIC
OCEAN

MS

Brazos River

LA

COASTAL

PLAIN

FL

TX

GULF

Mississippi
River Delta

Gulf of Mexico

Lake
Okeechobee

Everglades

BAHAMAS

Florida Keys

95°W 90°W 85°W 75°W

CUBA

CANADA

50°N
45°N
35°N
30°N
25°N

95°W 90°W 85°W 80°W 75°W 70°W 65°W

CANADA

NORTH DAKOTA
Grand Forks
Bismarck • Fargo
SOUTH DAKOTA
Pierre
Sioux Falls
NEBRASKA
Grand Island • ★Lincoln
Omaha

MINNESOTA
Duluth
Lake Superior
Marquette
MICHIGAN
WISCONSIN
St. Paul
Minneapolis
Green Bay
Madison
Milwaukee
IOWA
Cedar Rapids
Des Moines

Lake Huron
Lake Michigan
Grand Rapids
Lansing
Detroit
Toledo
Cleveland
Lake Erie

NEW HAMPSHIRE
VERMONT
Burlington
Montpelier • Portland
Concord ★ Manchester
NEW YORK
Albany ★
Rochester
Buffalo
MAINE
Presque Isle
Calais
★Augusta
Boston
MASSACHUSETTS
Hartford ★ Providence
New Haven **RHODE ISLAND**
CONNECTICUT
Newark • New York

KANSAS
Kansas City
Topeka
Dodge City • Wichita

Missouri River
Kansas City
Jefferson City
MISSOURI
St. Louis
Springfield

ILLINOIS **INDIANA**
Rockford
Chicago
South Bend
Indianapolis
Columbus
Cincinnati
OHIO
Louisville
Frankfort
Lexington

PENNSYLVANIA
Pittsburgh
Harrisburg
Baltimore
Washington, D.C. ⊛
WEST VIRGINIA
Charleston
Richmond ★
VIRGINIA

Trenton **NEW JERSEY**
Philadelphia
Dover **DELAWARE**
Annapolis
MARYLAND
Norfolk

OKLAHOMA
Enid
Tulsa
Oklahoma ★ City
Fort Smith

ARKANSAS
Little Rock ★
Memphis
TENNESSEE
★Nashville
Bowling Green
Knoxville
Chattanooga

Ohio River
Mississippi River

KENTUCKY
Winston-Salem • Greensboro
Raleigh ★
NORTH CAROLINA
Wilmington

TEXAS
Fort Worth • Dallas
★Austin
Houston
San Antonio
Laredo
Corpus Christi
Brownsville

LOUISIANA
Shreveport
Jackson ★
Vicksburg
MISSISSIPPI
Tupelo
Birmingham
Montgomery ★
ALABAMA
Baton Rouge • Biloxi
New Orleans
Mobile

GEORGIA
★Atlanta
Valdosta
★Tallahassee
FLORIDA

SOUTH CAROLINA
★Columbia
Charleston
Savannah

Jacksonville
Orlando
Tampa
St. Petersburg
Ft. Myers
Fort Lauderdale
Miami

ATLANTIC OCEAN

Gulf of Mexico

BAHAMAS

CUBA

95°W 90°W 85°W 75°W

State Abbreviation Chart

State Abbreviation	State	Date Entered Union	State Abbreviation	State	Date Entered Union
AK	Alaska	1959	MT	Montana	1889
AL	Alabama	1819	NC	North Carolina	1789
AR	Arkansas	1836	ND	North Dakota	1889
AZ	Arizona	1912	NE	Nebraska	1867
CA	California	1850	NH	New Hampshire	1788
CO	Colorado	1876	NJ	New Jersey	1787
CT	Connecticut	1788	NM	New Mexico	1912
DC	District of Columbia	1800	NV	Nevada	1864
DE	Delaware	1787	NY	New York	1788
FL	Florida	1845	OH	Ohio	1803
GA	Georgia	1788	OK	Oklahoma	1907
HI	Hawaii	1959	OR	Oregon	1859
IA	Iowa	1846	PA	Pennsylvania	1787
ID	Idaho	1890	RI	Rhode Island	1790
IL	Illinois	1818	SC	South Carolina	1788
IN	Indiana	1816	SD	South Dakota	1889
KS	Kansas	1861	TN	Tennessee	1796
KY	Kentucky	1792	TX	Texas	1845
LA	Louisiana	1812	UT	Utah	1896
MA	Massachusetts	1788	VT	Vermont	1791
MD	Maryland	1788	VA	Virginia	1788
ME	Maine	1820	WA	Washington	1889
MI	Michigan	1837	WI	Wisconsin	1848
MN	Minnesota	1858	WV	West Virginia	1863
MO	Missouri	1821	WY	Wyoming	1890
MS	Mississippi	1817			

Credits

EDITORIAL DEVELOPMENT AND PRODUCT MANAGEMENT

Product Development: *Charles Regan, Vice President, Maps.com*

Product Manager: *Martin Walz*

Content Writer: *Betsy Hedberg*

Design, Production, and Illustration: *Bill Hansen*

Editor: *John Holdren, Director of Content and Curriculum, K12 Inc.*

Editor: *Patricia Pearson, History Content Specialist, K12 Inc.*

Editorial Consultant: *John G. Agnone, Director of Publications and Media, K12 Inc.*

Editorial Consultant: *Luke Ohrn*

Clean Reader: *Bud Knecht, Senior Editor, K12 Inc.*

Maps: *Maps.com (Martha Bostwick - Lead Cartographer), Martin Walz*

PHOTOGRAPHS

page 7 Jupiter images / Liquid library; **page 9** Library of Congress; **page 12** Jupiter images / Liquid library (top), Dynamic Graphics (bottom); **page 15** Corbis images (top), Lonely Planet Images, *John Elk III* (bottom); **page 18** Library of Congress; **page 20** Dynamic Graphics (left), Jupiter images / Liquid library (right); **page 23** Corbis images (top), Lonely Planet Images, *Peter Ptschelinzew* (bottom); **page 24** Corbis images; **page 27** Lonely Planet Images *Jim Wark*; **page 28** Dynamic Graphics (top), Jupiter images / Liquid library (bottom); **page 29** Jupiter images / Liquid library; **page 31** Jupiter images / Liquid library; **page 36** Jupiter images / Liquid library (top), Lonely Planet Images, *Lee Foster* (bottom); **page 37** Jupiter images / Liquid library; **page 41** Lonely Planet Images, *Lee Foster*; **page 47** Jupiter images / Liquid library; **page 50** Lonely Planet Images, *Lee Foster*; **page 51** Library of Congress; **page 53** Library of Congress, *Theodore Horydczak*; **page 54** Dynamic Graphics (right), Jupiter images / Liquid library (left); **page 55** Jupiter images / Liquid library; **page 57** Jupiter images / Liquid library